Also by Tina B. Tessina, Ph.D.

It Ends with You: Grow Up and Out of Dysfunction

The Real Thirteenth Step: Achieving Autonomy, Confidence, and Self-Reliance beyond the Twelve-Step Programs, Revised

The Ten Smartest Decisions a Woman Can Make After Forty

The Unofficial Guide to Dating Again

Gay Relationships: How to Find Them, How to Improve Them, How to Make Them Last

Lovestyles: How to Celebrate Your Differences

With Riley K. Smith

How to Be a Couple and Still Be Free

Equal Partners

True Partners

With Elizabeth Friar Williams

The 10 Smartest Decisions a Woman Can Make Before 40

Money, Sex, and Kids

MONEY SEX AND KIDS

Stop Fighting about the Three Things That Can Ruin Your Marriage

TINA B. TESSINA, PH.D.

Aadamsmedia
Avon, Massachusetts

Published by Adams Media, an F+W Publications Company
57 Littlefield Street
Avon, MA 02322
www.adamsmedia.com

ISBN-10: 1-59869-325-5
ISBN-13: 978-1-59869-325-6

Library of Congress Cataloging-in-Publication Data
is available from the publisher

Printed in Canada

J I H G F E D C B A

This publication is designed to provide accurate and authoritative
information with regard to the subject matter covered. It is sold with
the understanding that the publisher is not engaged in rendering
legal, accounting, or other professional advice. If legal advice or other
expert assistance is required, the services of a competent professional
person should be sought.

—From a *Declaration of Principles* jointly adopted by a
Committee of the American Bar Association and
a Committee of Publishers and Associations

Many of the designations used by manufacturers and sellers to dis-
tinguish their product are claimed as trademarks. Where those
designations appear in this book and Adams Media was aware of
a trademark claim, the designations have been printed with initial
capital letters.

This book is available at quantity discounts for bulk purchases.
For imformation, please call 1-800-289-0963.

This book is dedicated to my husband,
Richard N. Sharrard, who inspires and teaches
me every day of our lives together.
Happy 25th anniversary!

CONTENTS

ACKNOWLEDGMENTS

Thanks go to my husband of twenty-five years, Richard Sharrard, who supports me through all the stress of writing, and whom I admire as one of the kindest, most caring men on the planet. If you're Richard's friend or neighbor, you're a blessed person, because he cares, and shows he does. And that generosity is even more present at home.

Laurie Harper has been my sole literary agent since 1995, and I'm not the only one who calls her my "guardian agent." She has been the force behind my career, helping me time and time again to reshape proposals into successful sellers, presenting me to new publishers and supporting me through the writing process. I have been blessed to share these years with her, and I'm looking forward to many more. Laurie can tell the truth as clearly as necessary, yet be kind when doing it. In Umberto Eco's words, she is "God in plain clothes," helping me and others clarify and shape ideas into publishable product.

I couldn't write much without the support of my chosen family, in (more or less) alphabetical order: Isadora Alman, Maggie and Ed Bialack, Victoria Bryan and Carrie Williams, Sylvia and Glen McWilliams, and Riley K. Smith. All of you really know what friends are for, and I am surrounded by love, laughter, and caring because of you. Also to Beverly Terfloth, who has comforted me with tea and sympathy at the Vintage Tea Leaf, and Cindy Cyr Atkinson and the staff at The Coffee Cup, my other writer's hangout.

Thanks also to my editor at Adams, Paula Munier, who had the idea for the book and believed I could write it, and who made such wonderful editorial suggestions. It's rare to find an editor who treats your work with such respect. And to her assistant, Brendan O'Neill, who was always there to answer a question or to clarify a point. And to the staff at Adams Media, who support and encourage me.

Introduction

FROM STRUGGLING
TO SOLVING

Why did you pick up *Money, Sex, and Kids?* Your interest in this book says you are married, you recognized some issues that have challenged your own marriage, and you're looking for help, information, and solutions. Above all, you're looking for a book that is written for women and men who repeatedly struggle with the same issues—sex, money, and children. In over thirty years of couples counseling, I have frequently worked with couples who fight about family, who's right, housekeeping issues, and time. They often resort to yelling and blaming. In these pages, you will find the solutions I have developed to eliminate these fights. This book will teach you what you need to know to build the healthy, loving partnership you want. Healthy relationships are built on a foundation of clear thinking, problem solving, and mutual support. Any willing couple can learn to build a happy relationship if they stop reacting and learn to respond thoughtfully.

As an individual you have ideas and beliefs about how certain things in life should be handled and so does your partner, and we all tend to assume everyone, especially a person who loves us, will see it our way. While dating, you two may have felt that you agreed with each other on everything. But after you married, things changed. You were probably shocked when you realized the object of your affections, your dream come true, the Prince or Princess Charming you fell in love with, had different ideas about how life, love, home, finances, and children should be handled.

In my practice over the years, I've spent many hours teaching couples the techniques and information that will allow them to communicate and solve problems, rather than fight endlessly about the same things. In twenty-five years of marriage, I've also learned from my own experience that there's a big difference between the skills and attitudes needed to date and fall in love and what is needed to make married life work smoothly. There's a difference between being lovers and being partners, and on top of all that, keeping enough romance and fun alive to make it all feel worthwhile. Those of us who succeed are the blessed ones, the happy ones, and you can be, too.

In this book, you'll learn to view your relationship as a partnership, rather than a challenge or a competition, and you'll discover new ways to think about sharing and working together to make all your decisions about money, sex, and kids mutual ones. With a little information and practice, you can become a successful, happy couple. The point of this book is to show you how to create a partnership that will cause you to feel blessed and happy.

How This Book Is Organized

Chapter 1 is an overview of why couples argue to give you an idea of what we're going to cover in the remaining chapters. The next three chapters have a brief introduction and then present the main issues that create conflict about money, sex, or kids. Each subject is divided into the main issues about the chapter topic, and each issue is presented with a section called "Struggle" which introduces the problem and gives a case history of a couple who are arguing about it. The next section, called "Situation" describes how and why this couple, and couples in general, fights about the topic. A third, "Solution," section presents the way to solve the problems and resolve the conflict. You will be able to read the book cover to cover for a thorough discussion and presentation of all the problems, or skip around and find whichever problems are most prevalent in your relationship. By understanding the reasons behind your arguments, and implementing the solutions, you can move from struggle to solution in your own marriage.

From chapter 5 through the rest of the book, you'll learn to understand why you and your partner argue and the remaining skills you need to enhance your relationship and transform your struggles into working together to create a smoothly working partnership.

With this book, you'll be able to resolve your issues about money, sex, and kids, and move on to having a workable, satisfying relationship, with minimal or no arguing or fighting.

Chapter 1

THE THREE BIG TEMPTATIONS

How often have you heard yourself and your spouse make these complaints about each other:

- "You don't listen."
- "You spend too much money."
- "You never want to have sex."
- "You're always at work; you never come home to spend time with the family."
- "You're too harsh with the kids."
- "You let the kids do whatever they want."

If you and your spouse are fighting about or struggling with these issues, you are not alone. In my counseling practice, I see many couples, much like you, voicing these complaints over and over.

In every marriage, the main struggles are similar: Like you, other couples also fight about money, sex, and kids, with fights about territory, power, and other people following close behind. If you're feeling tense, worried, stressed, upset, at your wit's end, and wanting help because you and your partner are fighting about these issues, you'll find help in these pages. Whether you're newly married or married for a long time; in your first, second, or even third marriage; with kids, planning kids, or with step-kids; and no matter what level of economic status—from just getting by to wealthy—you'll find the information and techniques you need here.

The Big Issues: Money, Sex, and Kids

Certain kinds of problems are more emotion-charged than others. I often ask my clients to stop and think about what they're doing in the middle of a fight, and ask them what they look like to themselves. They realize they sound and look like children fighting, and they're not making sense, even to themselves. The reason most people fight about money, sex, and kids is that these are the issues with the biggest emotional charge for most people, and they carry the most baggage from our early families. Let's look at some of the reasons why money, sex, and kids issues are so powerful and volatile in couple relationships.

Money

Money represents power and even attractiveness in our society. Furthermore, it may be charged with meaning it doesn't actually possess. I've discovered in working through these issues with clients that sometimes a client who grew up poor may unconsciously believe that rich people are mean or evil.

Dorothy and Bill are both in their late twenties, college educated, and they've been married for five years. It's a first marriage for each of them, and they're both well established in their careers. Dorothy is a human resources manager for a large corporation, and Bill is a sales manager for a software company. They have a lot in common because they grew up in similar, lower-income families with hardworking parents.

Dorothy, an attractive and successful businesswoman of twenty-eight, says: "My parents didn't have much money, but we were loved and well cared for. My father was one of the most admirable men I've ever met. He was the one who would help the elderly ladies down the church steps. But I saw it in church; the rich people sat together and had nothing to do with people like us. They looked down on my parents. I decided I didn't like anyone who was rich. Now, when my husband wants to buy a nice car, I fight with him about it, because I don't think it's right to show off."

Others believe that enough money will bring prestige, success, and happiness: Dorothy's husband, Bill, maintains:

"To succeed in business, I have to present myself well—I need a good car, nice suits, a Rolex watch, a Blackberry, and an expensive laptop. When others see me looking good, they will be more likely to trust me and want to make the deal."

Needless to say, Dorothy and Bill tend to struggle when it comes to budgeting, saving, and spending money. In chapter 2, you'll learn the techniques they used to solve these problems. Here are some money issues you and your partner may fight about:

- Who pays for what?
- Who keeps records, pays bills, controls the budget, and so on?
- When, how, and why do we spend money?
- One of you wants to save; the other wants to spend.
- How do you make big financial decisions?

Or, perhaps, you can't talk about money at all without arguing. If you and your partner tend to think the business end of a relationship is not a romantic topic for courtship, you may not discuss it until you can't avoid it, and then you fight.

You may not think of your marriage as a business deal, but a huge part of it is just that. Just like a business, a marriage takes in income, pays expenses, and is supposed to have a little profit (savings) left over. In the following chapters, you'll learn how to handle your finances like a smoothly run business, without the need for arguments.

Sex

Fights about sex usually appear to be about:

- How often you have it
- Who initiates it
- The way your sexual needs change as your relationship grows
- Fidelity and betrayal
- Losing interest in each other

Although these are the presenting issues, they are misleading. Under the surface, most couple fights are really about "do you love me?" Fighting about small details can be confusing, and confusion can intensify your doubts about being loved. Sex often involves a lot of anxiety, because everyone fears rejection and is trying to live up to the impossible standards set by media images. You and your partner are most vulnerable when it comes to sex, which is why sex is difficult to keep going in a relationship; when you get scared, you shut down and turn off. If you reject your partner even once, he or she may stop initiating or responding for fear of further rejection, until the problem is cleared up.

Jan and Ron are former high school sweethearts who married right after graduation, fifteen years ago. They have two children, Ron Jr., thirteen, and Julie, eleven. Jan works as a teacher's aide, and Ron is a building contractor, and their lives are very busy. The first several years of their marriage were happy, but lately, they've been bickering, and their sex life is nearly nonexistent. What can they do to re-establish the good feelings they used to have for each other?

"Sex was so easy when we first met." Ron says, "Now, we hardly get together at all. What happened to wanting to have sex? If I try to get close, she's never interested, and then we argue."

"I can't relax and enjoy sex when we never talk to each other. Ron comes home late from work, tired and cranky, we eat dinner while watching TV, and then it's bedtime and he wants sex. Well, it doesn't work that way for me—so when I say no, we fight, and lose even more sleep. It's a vicious cycle."

Sex is an extension of your couple communication, in physical rather than verbal form, and you can learn how to make it work. The exercises and guidelines in the following pages will help you, and you'll find out how Jan and Ron solved their sexual problem.

Parenting and Children

Having children creates extra pressure in your relationship because parenting is a demanding, exacting, and stressful enterprise. Parenting requires consistency and experience, and because extended families are often living far apart, help that used to be available for previous generations from parents and siblings may not be there for you.

Parenting fights are most likely about how your parents raised you, as opposed to the way your partner's parents raised him or her. You wind up having a power struggle about who's right and who's wrong, and no one can win because it's your family history against your partner's. In these days of divorce and remarriage; blended and stepfamilies fight about stepchildren: who disciplines, fairness, and different parenting rules.

You and your partner may make accusations like:

- "You don't help enough (or the right way) with the children."
- "You treat your children (or our children) better/worse than my children."

- "You don't love my children the way you love our children."

You and your spouse can struggle about children before they even exist: Do we want a baby? Should we adopt? Fertility treatments cause a lot of frustration, sexual problems, and disappointment, too.

Perhaps you are fighting about who disciplines:

Daisy and Mike were sweethearts in college and married right after graduation, with the support of both their families and a big celebration with all their friends. They had a "dream relationship" and high hopes for happiness. They've been married for fourteen years. Daisy is now thirty-five, Mike is thirty-eight, and they have three children in grammar school. Daisy worked as a teacher for the first couple of years but decided to be a stay-at-home mom when the children were born. She went back to teaching after all three children were in school. Mike works in a factory, and together they provide a good income for the family.

They are frequently happy together, but they fight about disciplining the kids: "You leave all the hard stuff for me—I have to be the 'bad guy' while you get to play with the kids," says Daisy, and her husband Mike retorts: "I'm away all day at the office, and I wasn't there when the problem happened—it's not reasonable to ask me to come home and instantly be Daddy the enforcer."

Or, about whether the punishment is too severe or fits the "crime":

Mike thinks Daisy punishes the kids too harshly and that her rules are too strict, so he undermines what she's doing, and then they fight about it.

Perhaps you had children before you had a chance to solidify your couple relationship, or the changes were confusing, and you never re-established your teamwork. Perhaps you already had children when you met and have had problems becoming an authoritative team in the kids' eyes. Or perhaps your disagreement is about whether or not to have children. No matter what your struggles, the techniques you learn in the following chapters will help you come to agreement and work as a team to raise your children. As you'll see, they helped Mike and Daisy.

Other Contentious Issues

While money, sex, and kids may be the three most prevalent issues that cause couple dissension, there are some other issues that frequently appear in my office. Let's consider a few of those.

Territory

You may not feel as if you're competing for anything, but as a human, you are a territorial animal—without realizing it, you get just as protective of your personal space, physical and psychological, as the neighborhood cats do. You're just not as obvious about it. You are fighting for territory when you argue about these questions:

- How do you care for your living space (e.g., fights about "I'm neat, and you're sloppy" or styles of furnishing)? Who cleans house or does what chores, and who sets the standards for cleaning?
- How do you use time (struggles over one of you being late, the other on time)?
- How do you spend your recreational time? One of you may be more social and the other more physically active, or one wants to watch TV and the other wants to go out. What do you do together, and what separately?

- How do you divide space? Your mess is invading my space; I need alone time, and you're always here. Do we move for my job or yours?
- Privacy is another territorial issue. Can we open one another's mail, listen in on phone calls, do we share everything, or keep secrets?

Whenever your arguments are about these issues, your territorial instincts are getting in the way of your relationship. It is how you handle these situations that makes the difference.

Expectations about how all these things are handled begin in early childhood, before we know how to think about them, and so they are actually learned as prejudices—the right way to do it, rather than what works best. If you and your mate grew up in different styles, you can wind up having huge fights, the object of which is who's right and who's wrong. In the following chapters, you'll learn how to resolve these issues and develop a new, mutual style of your own.

Other People

A frequent source of trouble in today's relationships can be other people. Couples fight over whether friends can come over, who can come over, and when. Jealousy, interference, or problems caused by relatives and in-laws and which family you spend holidays with are all popular subjects for fights. In-law fights may be about "my family is better than yours," which is another version of "I'm right and you're wrong." It's a power struggle. Can we have friends from single days? Do all our friends have to be couples? Can I go out with the guys or gals? It's not easy for couples to resolve differences about how to handle all the other people in their lives. This book will teach you how to broach the subject, resolve your differences, and handle problems as they arise.

Symbolic Arguments

Sometimes there's no good reason why you're fighting about money or sex or kids. It may be a symbolic argument. It's not really about who's spending what, it's about fairness or respect. It's not really about helping with parenting; it's about whether you care about how hard your partner works. It definitely helps to let your partner know what the symbolic meaning is to you and for you to listen to your spouse's feelings about it. Does it feel unmanly and belittling to him to do housework? What if he's allergic, and raising dust gives him a couple of hours of sinus problems? These struggles are only insurmountable if you don't understand why you're arguing or what you're really arguing about.

To discover what the fight is really about, you need to talk. You'll learn techniques and discover guidelines to show you how to begin and how to uncover the underlying factors. For example,

- Why does he want it done the way he does?
- How does she think it should be?
- What do I really want?

Once you find out the specific reasons behind your own and your partner's preferences, you'll find out how to solve the problems you didn't know were there. Is there a concrete reason (it's more convenient this way, it saves money, it suits your personality) or is it just what you learned from Mom and Dad? Or is it a reaction against Mom and Dad? Is there a specific reason why not? Once you understand each other's reasons, you'll have an easier time coming up with a solution.

As you read through this book, you'll find guidelines and exercises designed to help you understand the concepts more fully. The exercises will let you experience how the information will help you overcome old habit patterns and change the way you and your spouse are relating. These tools, which have been tested in my counseling office, are designed as simple, step-by-step processes you can use to practice new techniques and information in your everyday life. They are easy to understand yet very effective at creating new ways for you to cope with your marriage issues. Exercises generally contain steps to follow, while guidelines are general suggestions for how to frame your thoughts or habits to increase your success. For example, the following exercise will help you begin breaking free from the prejudices, expectations, and assumptions that can cause strife in your relationship.

EXERCISE: Reframing

Step 1: Break free from your preset notions and biases by exercising your ability to come up with options.

Several seminal thinkers in psychology have suggested that any existential problem has five possible solutions, and if you haven't thought of five options, you haven't thought enough. Clinician trainer Denton Roberts jokes that the options are "Fight, Fornicate, Fool around, Fix it, or Forget it." There's a lot of wisdom in that quip. Here's how to use this wisdom in your present relationship.

If you're arguing, try calling "time out" and seeing if you can come up with five or six different ways you could handle the problem. The options don't have to be sensible; in fact if you crack a few jokes, it might lighten up the intensity of the argument. "That's it! I'm . . .

- Joining the space program
- Running away from home
- Calling for my mommy
- Hiding under the covers
- Taking Prozac

... to get away from problems like this!"

It can make both of you laugh, and get you back into a more companionable attitude.

Step 2: If your partner has said or done something that upset, hurt, or angered you, and you think you know what your partner intended by the remark or action, think of at least five other possible motivations or meanings before acting.
For example:

• He didn't intend it to sound the way you heard it.
• She was irritated by the children, not by you.
• He had some bad news you haven't heard yet.
• She was just joking or teasing.
• He himself was hurt or angered by something you said or did before.

Taking the time to think about other options will free you from the automatic, emotional responses that lead to conflict.

Problems with Problems
When your relationship is not going well, you probably don't have the confidence or experience to solve problems creatively, and you don't realize how important your relationship issues are, so you drift along, trying to deal with life on a day-to-day basis. When a crisis occurs, you are completely unprepared to solve it. Therapists describe a relationship that doesn't function properly as *dysfunctional*. This means it isn't working (functioning) the way it should.
The basic functions of a healthy relationship are:

• Communication
• Problem solving

- Mutual support
- Shared responsibility
- Establishing financial security
- Providing emotional warmth

When these functions aren't working, communication shuts down, all connections between the partners (including sex) falter, discussions become struggles, and the level of discontent and frustration rises.

No matter what you're fighting about—money, sex, kids, or something else—the fighting is an indication that your communication isn't working. If this happens only occasionally, such as when one or both of you are tired or stressed; it's not too big a problem. However, if you argue or bicker on a daily or weekly basis, or you keep fighting about the same thing over and over, then your communication is not functioning as it should and you don't know how to move from a problem to the solution. When this happens, problems are recurrent, endless, and possibly exaggerated into relationship disasters.

Discontent and frustration are destructive because they give rise to hopelessness and despair. If you and your partner can't solve problems, communicate, or get along, both of you will lose hope that you will ever be able to enjoy each other or life together. When you're frustrated and hopeless, you lack patience and the ability to think clearly and creatively. The good news is, you can learn patience and clear thinking.

Acquiring Patience

Learning to be patient and remain calm reduces and relieves stress and worry. Cultivating patience is really learning to manage impulses—it's an issue in self-control. You can learn how to do "emotional maintenance" and shake off stress, keep on track of what you want to do, and let go of frustration when something is getting to you. Patience is learning how to wait until you've thought before acting. It's making sure you understand the options and take control of your own ideas and decisions. It's a growth process, a transformation of self through awareness and learning.

To acquire patience, learn not to act on impulse, change your thinking and attitude, and reach out for support and encouragement. The following seven steps will help you gain the necessary patience and determination to enhance your communication.

EXERCISE: Seven Steps to Help You Learn Patience

1. Wait: The old advice to "count to ten before you respond" is a great way to learn patience. Give yourself a chance to give your best response.

2. Use perspective: Put your impulses or desires in perspective. Will it be important an hour from now—fifteen minutes from now? Most of them won't be.

3. Understand yourself: If you are tempted to act or speak on impulse, understand that the impulse is normal, but you don't have to be ruled by it. Reactions and impulses are normal—it's how thoughtfully we act on them that counts.

4. Take a longer view: If you're reacting because someone upset you (e.g., your partner hurt your feelings), then give a little prayer of thanks that it wasn't worse; say a blessing for your partner (who probably needs it), and you'll feel better. If you are tempted to act impulsively, pause a minute and consider your bigger goal—then decide if the momentary impulse is worth setting back your goal.

5. Give yourself a break: If you act on an impulse before thinking about it, acknowledge that you did it, then forgive yourself and get back on track. If you find yourself acting impulsively a lot, then maybe your goal is too rigid. Maybe you need to allow a little more room for yourself or to renegotiate the contract with your spouse. (See the following section on expectations.)

6. Consider the source: Impulses are often a reaction to outside circumstances—for example, being annoyed because your partner isn't available although you could enjoy using the time you have to yourself. Make sure what you do is what you really want to do.

7. Celebrate: Remember to celebrate your accomplishments and all the times you did what you intended to, kept your promises, and worked things out. Frequent small celebrations are a way to reward yourself for patience and to increase your motivation to be even more patient.

Disappointment and Expectations

We all have high hopes and rosy pictures of the future when we enter a new relationship, so when life turns out not to be perfect and you find out your partner actually is an imperfect human, just like you, it's disappointing. You may begin by expecting that your partner will always see your point of view or that as long as you love each other, everything will be OK, but after a while, reality breaks through and you realize your expectations were unrealistic. If you feel you're constantly disappointed and frequently angry, consider that it may be because your expectations don't line up with reality.

No matter how little reality resembles your dreams, there's no need to argue about it. We all deal with many disappointments in daily life, at home, and at work. In most cases, neither you nor your partner would argue with the boss, colleagues at work, or a child's teacher the way you argue with each other. In domestic situations, you can choose your behavior in the same way—you don't have to argue with each other. Instead of acting like bickering children, use your grownup self-control to pull yourself out of the argument. If you're fighting over silly little things, remember you're having symbolic fights—it's not really about who didn't put the cap on the toothpaste, it's about disappointment, who is right, who has the most power, who deserves to be loved.

Guidelines for Not Fighting

1. Don't participate: Disagreements always require two people. If you don't participate, your partner can't argue without you. If the issue arises at an inopportune time, you can just find a temporary resolution (temporarily give in, go home, leave the restaurant) and wait until things calm down to discuss what happened (the argument may just have been a case of too much alcohol, or being tired and irritable.) Then talk about what you can do instead if it ever happens again.

2. Discuss recurring problems: To resolve recurring problems, discuss related decisions with your spouse and find out what each of you does and does not want before making important decisions. You have a lot of options; so don't let confusion add to the stress.

3. Seek to understand: Make sure you and your partner understand each other's point of view before beginning to solve the problem. You should be able to put your mate's position in your own words, and vice versa. This does not mean that you agree with each other, just that you understand each other. (There will be more information about how to understand in later chapters.)

4. Solve it for the two of you: Come up with a solution that works for just the two of you, ignoring anyone else's needs. It's much easier to solve a problem for the two of you than for others you may not understand. After you are clear with each other, discuss the issues with others who may be involved.

5. Talk to others: If extended family members or friends might have problems with your decision, talk about what objections they might have, so you can defuse them beforehand. Discuss possible ways to handle their objections.

Arguments often occur because you're following automatic habit patterns that lead to a problem before you know it. Using these guidelines will help you overcome negative habit patterns you may have built that lead to arguments or bickering.

How Patterns Develop

If you understand how habit patterns develop, how strong they are, and what to do about them, you can see mistakes as they happen, or even before you make them, and change what you're doing. Research shows that people unconsciously look for behavior patterns to follow, and once a pattern is established, they tend to follow it unconsciously. Think about when you change jobs or homes, and how difficult it is for the first couple of weeks to remember to drive in the new direction, and you'll get an idea of how strong patterns are. The same thing happens in your relationship.

Each first event in dating and marriage creates a pattern you are likely to follow, unless you become aware and consciously change the habits that are problematic. Doing what you've always done is easy, and it reduces stress when it works well. It is only when the old familiar pattern leads to problems that it creates stress. Planning your wedding, for example, creates patterns for dealing with extended family, solving problems together, making financial decisions, and being considerate of each other's feelings. Your first fight lays down a pattern for all future fights, so if you calm down, solve the problem and then make up, you've created a useful format to follow. These patterns are like the first layer of bricks in a wall. Every later brick will build on the pattern laid down at first, so if some of the patterns you've developed in your early relationship are creating problems, it's worth the effort to learn to change them.

We also acquire patterns and habits from our early family and from past relationships. If you have created a habit of fighting instead of working things out, the good news is you can correct them. Maybe you bought the dream: You and this wonderful partner would get married, make a life together, have some really great kids, and life would be wonderful. That's how the romantic movies and happy sitcoms show it, isn't it? But, on some days, maybe your relationship feels more like *The War of the Roses*, and you despair of ever working it out.

There's no need for despair; in thirty years of marriage counseling, I've found almost any problem in a relationship can be fixed if both partners want to fix it. What gets in the way is lack of skills and destructive patterns that get set up in the first months and years of your relationship. In the following chapters, we'll examine the major relationship problems, and I'll teach you the skills you need to overcome them and work out future problems without fighting.

Shared Responsibility

In my counseling office, I see many couples who are confused about responsibility. Either one or both partners think the responsibilities aren't properly shared. Relationship responsibility is rarely discussed in movies and on TV. In romantic movies, the chores just seem to get done, no one ever talks about paying bills, and when we do see the couple in a domestic situation, they're either romantically cooking dinner together or cuddling in front of the fire. But your real relationship involves lots of responsibility. Not only do the two of you have all the responsibilities you did when you were single (keeping house; paying bills; maintaining your personal health, hygiene, and clothing; caring for pets, children, or other family members; working at your career; going to school and/or running a business), but you also have some new responsibilities *to each other*. For example, once you are in a relationship, you are responsible for communicating to each other about schedules, feelings, what you want, how you want to do things, and future plans. You also have a responsibility to consider each other's wants and needs as well as your own. Decisions you made on your own as a single person now must be discussed and often negotiated, or at least communicated. You may have additional responsibilities toward your partner's friends and relatives, too. Life can become much more complicated, and more difficult to manage.

When you both understand your individual and mutual responsibilities, and plan together to handle them effectively, you can work as a team, and actually reduce the amount of stress and labor involved. If you have misunderstandings or disagreements about your responsibilities, and struggle with each other about them, the amount of stress can increase dramatically. It's very helpful, at any point in your relationship, to discuss your individual and mutual obligations and responsibilities and reach agreements that you can keep. The following tips will help you learn to communicate about and solve the distribution of responsibility rather than struggle and compete.

Communication Tips

Here are four tips for keeping the communication open in your relationship:

1. Talk frequently and honestly to each other about your frustrations, about sex, about anger, about disappointment, about your appreciation of each other, about the meaning of life, about everything. Instead of setting up a system of division of labor and locking it in stone, talk frequently about how you feel, what's fair, what you're tired of doing, and what you'd like to change. Don't forget to talk about the positives, thank each other, and mention what's going well.

2. Strive to work together to solve anything that comes up, and build teamwork and partnership together. Don't get stuck on who's right or wrong. Instead, focus on what will solve the problem. Talk about the problem, such as unequal responsibility, only long enough to define and understand it, and then switch your attention to solutions that work for both of you.

3. Keep your connection going through communication, sex, affection, understanding, and concern for each other. Connect every day in some meaningful way, even if all you can manage is a note, a phone conversation, an instant message or e-mail. Part of your responsibility is to keep your relationship healthy by making sure your love for each other is visible and accessible.

4. Have a sense of humor, give the benefit of the doubt, and care about each other. When responsibilities and stress increase—especially when something difficult happens, like an illness, financial problem, or unforeseen problem—your teamwork should increase also. Think about what you can do to make any difficult situation easier for each other. This is the best time to praise each other, thank each other, and remind each other of your love. Later in this book, you'll learn many tools for creating partnership and healthy communication.

Solving Instead of Struggling

According to researcher John Gottman and several other studies, couples who can solve problems successfully together tend to have relationships that last. If you've been through a tough time together, then you're probably frustrated, hurt, and anxious. This erodes your patience and reasonableness with each other, and makes it difficult to think clearly.

Successful couples don't have any special magic. By trial and error, through counseling, books, and talking to other couples, they figure out how to create a relationship that works. To create a working partnership, you need to teach each other how to understand one another so you can get along. When you're working together or spending time with each other, instead of complaining, criticizing, or resenting each other, try asking each other what you're thinking about the situation. "I think it would work better to do this—what do you think?" If you listen to each other, and focus on sharing what you know, you'll grow in understanding and teamwork. Most partners would rather have each other's company than do it all alone, especially if what you're doing is new and if it's companionable company. The best way to end the "who is supposed to do what" argument is to do it (or at least work it out) together and make it fun. A smart partner will make this as easy as possible—make it fun and affectionate, and focus on becoming a team. Rather than figure out who's right, couples need to focus on what works, and find ways to motivate each other to work together.

Celebration + Appreciation = Motivation

Motivation comes from celebration and appreciation. When partners get frustrated, they have a tendency to complain to and criticize each other rather than appreciate each other. If you give in to your urge to criticize, you'll mortally wound your marriage. If you want to motivate each other, you need to share as much appreciation and celebration as possible. Work with each other, thank each other, and make doing the work as much fun as possible.

You Can Stop Fighting

If you've had a difficult time with each other, I'm sorry, and I know you're frustrated, but if you will renew your patience, start working together to fix the problems, and give the information and exercises in this book a couple of months, you will see results. Most of the couples I counsel succeed in fixing their problems, and you can, too. If you're reading this book, that means you're looking for a solution, and that's a big step toward success.

In subsequent chapters of this book, you'll learn how to change focus from fighting over money, sex, and kids to developing the ability to talk about what is going on and focus on solving the problem, which leaves a lot more time for having fun and getting things done. Any willing couple can learn to build a happy relationship—and so can *you*.

Chapter 2

SOLVING MONEY SQUABBLES

U.S. News & World Report recently had a cover title: "Till Debt Do Us Part." They chose this focus to sell magazines because a recent study discovered that the number one topic couples fight about is financial issues. Why money? Because money is symbolic of so many emotionally charged issues. In our society, money represents power, success, and often even your value as a person. We say (misquoting the Bible,) "Money is the root of all evil" or "money is power." We consider it spiritual to take a vow of poverty, and we prosecute and convict people who get greedy. Money is serious stuff. Some of us think people who make a lot of money must lack character; others think poor people are morally deficient. These attitudes are not the way we want to think, they're prejudices, acquired before we learned to think rationally.

STRUGGLE
Different Money Attitudes

Whether you are aware of it or not, your attitudes about money (among other things) are unconsciously learned in early childhood. When you think about it objectively, money is a simple piece of paper or bank account balance that represents what you've earned through work or investment, a means of transforming your labor into an easily portable way to buy what you want. But in emotional terms, money becomes symbolic of many different things. You can see it as a substitute for or expression of love, power, self-worth, social status, security, intelligence, fear, or ethics.

Your early experiences, beliefs, and prejudices about money affect the way you deal with it today, and the same is true of your spouse or partner. This is why what should be a simple discussion of earning, spending, and planning for the future can quickly flare into a war.

Let's look at some of the things each of you may have learned in your early family and how they might affect your thoughts and actions as an adult, and also your difficulties in your marriage.

Scarcity

If your childhood was spent in difficult, poverty-ridden circumstances, a political or war situation where money and food were scarce, or some other experience of want, you can grow up with a consciousness of scarcity and anxiety about money. Some relatively poor families manage to avoid creating anxiety in their children by making careful choices and creating a loving, warm, supportive environment; but the child may grow up with a sense of inequity anyway, as Dorothy (of Dorothy and Bill, the twenty-something, two-career couple we met in the first chapter) did.

"I don't remember feeling deprived because we were poor—my family was a happy one. But I do remember watching the wealthy people in church look down at my wonderful, caring father, who always shared what he had and helped others, because they knew he was just a poor janitor. They treated him with disrespect. Now, although Bill and I are very comfortable, and I was able to take care of my parents as they got older, I'm really careful not to show off possessions or have too fancy a car. I buy my clothes at inexpensive places."

Dorothy's husband, Bill, on the other hand, grew up in similar circumstances to his wife—a low-income family on the poor side of town. Bill says, "I've done well, and I take pride in showing that I've come a long way from my roots. Driving a fancy car is important to me; it makes me feel good. I want to live in a big house in an upscale neighborhood. I think wearing designer clothes helps me make a better impression at work." Dorothy and Bill, as you might suspect, often argue about how to spend money, and keeping up with the neighbors and co-workers."

Lack of money in childhood can lead to a feeling of desperation about making money as an adult and the feeling that there's never enough money. Legendary *Cosmopolitan* magazine editor Helen Gurley Brown's comment "You can never be too rich" may come from this kind of childhood, as well as the need for very ostentatious spending and "bling" among sports stars, celebrities, and musicians who grew up rough. A childhood experience of scarcity may cause you to be very successful, driven, and focused on earning money; or it can defeat you, causing you to feel unworthy and incapable of financial success.

Love or Approval

If money was used to show love or approval in childhood, as an adult you may give overly lavish presents and try to "buy" love and friendship, or you may only value others who have a lot of money. You may only feel good about yourself when you are making lots of money, and your family may complain that you buy them a lot but they'd rather you spent time with them. Former college sweethearts Mike and Daisy, married for fourteen years, have frequently struggled about money differences.

In childhood, Daisy was rewarded with money for every good grade on her report card, given a generous allowance, and lavished with presents on her birthday and Christmas. Both of her parents worked, and had more money than time, and she often felt that it was more acceptable to ask for things than for time. Her husband, Mike, had a stay-at-home mom, who spent a lot of time helping him with school projects, cooking, and baking. Mike says: "Even though Daisy and I both work, we struggle about spending money. Daisy wants to go out to eat, I want to stay home and cook. She wants something flashy for Christmas, I want something useful, and both of us get what we don't want. I want to save to buy a home; Daisy wants to spend money now. It's a constant battle. I want to spend time relaxing at home; Daisy wants to go somewhere that costs money."

Power

If money determined who won when you were young—for example, your father was the major wage earner and your mother always deferred to him, you might grow up to feel that the amount of money you have determines your position in life. Or, perhaps you were in a situation where there were obvious differences between the haves and have-nots, and no matter which side you were on, you may have been impressed with the power and importance of having money. The recent stories of top executives who cheat and steal funds are illustrations of people who would do anything for more money, and who view money as necessary for personal power.

Lucy, age forty, and Greg, forty-five, have been married fifteen years, and they have two teenage children. Lucy has been a stay-at-home mom for most of their marriage, and Greg owns his own insurance agency.

Because Lucy is a stay-at-home mom whose kids are now teenagers, she has not earned much money, and her husband Greg has worked all of their married life. Greg and Lucy struggle over who has the right to decide how their money is spent. Lucy says, "Greg makes financial decisions without consulting me, and then I get angry and spend money to 'get even.' We fight about money all the time."

Social Status

If you grew up in poverty, or as a member of a minority group, you might unconsciously view money as a symbol for social acceptability and self-esteem. As an adult, you might be focused on fashionable, expensive brand names, status symbols such as extravagant cars and palatial homes. Sometimes the need for these prestigious possessions and ostentatious spending leads to massive debt, or white-collar crime. The recent corporate and political scandals demonstrate what happens when people are willing to do anything to get money, and when no amount of money is ever enough. When one or both partners use money to establish social status and self-worth, fights will be about "what the neighbors think" and "keeping up with the Joneses."

Harold, thirty-eight, and Cassandra, thirty-three, are both lawyers. They've been married for seven years. He graduated from Yale Law School, and she from the University of Michigan, where her family lived. Cassandra was the first in her family to get a college education and to work as a professional, and she lacks some self-confidence as a result. Harold, on the other hand, was privileged from childhood, and takes his status for granted. He says, "Cassandra takes offense so easily, I never know what will set her off. If I try to discuss whether her desire to purchase a more expensive car makes sense, she immediately says 'You don't think I deserve it.' We have plenty of money, a lovely house in a great neighborhood, and two prestigious careers. I just don't understand what's wrong."

Security and Comfort

If money was used as a way to feel better in childhood and your parents said, "Poor baby, your friend hurt your feelings? Let's go buy you a new toy and you'll feel better." You might grow up to use money as a way to avoid feelings of fear, hurt, anger, or grief, which could make you vulnerable to a shopping or gambling addiction. If you've ever said you are using "retail therapy" as a humorous way of saying you're shopping to soothe yourself, this might be your style.

Dirk, thirty-five, and Cheryl, twenty-eight, have only been married for two years. Dirk has a relatively new business as an electrical contractor, and Cheryl works as a receptionist. Cheryl and Dirk recognized each other immediately when they met—they had so much in common—similar childhoods, and a lot of shared experience. They each gave the other a nice present on their second date. Cheryl says: "Whenever one of us has a difficult day, we make a date to go out for an expensive dinner, and after a tough week, we might buy something new for the house." The problem with this is, they can't afford it, and they have incurred massive credit card debt trying to soothe themselves. "Now," says Cheryl, "we blame each other for the difficulty we're in."

SITUATION

Emotion about Difference

Each of these couples has problems with money, and they all fight about it. They need to learn new attitudes about finances, what money is for, and how to use it.

If you absorbed a healthy attitude toward money from your childhood family and learned how to save it, when and how to spend it appropriately and wisely, and how to use it as the tool it really is, you'll most likely feel comfortable with money and have less emotional charge about saving, spending, sharing, or using it. If not, you can still learn new approaches with money and stop arguing about it.

Understanding that money issues are a real problem that can lead to divorce, taking them seriously, and learning how not to fight about them will make a big difference in your chances for success as a married couple. Taking steps to calm the money miscues can go a long way to preventing problems in your relationship.

Marriage Is a Financial Institution

The business aspects of marriage are clear to me, because for fifteen years before I went back to school and eventually became licensed as a therapist, I was an accountant in business. Just like a small business, your relationship has one or more sources of income, you have expenses, and, like a business, your marriage is supposed to make a profit—to create savings, investments, and equity (which a business would call assets) and have money left over in the bank at the end of the month. As partners in a marriage you have financial responsibilities similar to those of partners in a business. In fact, some businesses are called partnerships, and we often use the same word for relationships. Family members are somewhat like workers when they do maintenance, chores, and homework, and somewhat like clients who receive services from the partners, Mom and Dad. Mom and Dad are the chief operating and financial officers, who must figure out how to allocate the funds coming in, and how to provide the necessary guidance and services to their children and to each other. In business, there's a lot of discussion about "corporate culture," that is, the attitudes and practices within the business: how employees and executives deal with each other; the ethics of the company; and their focus, or lack thereof, on meeting goals and becoming successful. Likewise, your marriage and family have a "family culture"—how you interact as partners and family members; your mutual goals, hopes, and dreams; and how successful or unsuccessful you are at meeting your goals. Obviously, a family culture that involves a lot of fighting about money will be less efficient and not as successful at meeting its goals.

No matter what your circumstances, creating financial security can make life easier. To do this, you must learn to manage your money wisely. The amount of money you bring in may not be large, but if you manage it well, it can be all you need. On the other hand, we have all heard stories of people who brought in vast sums of money (lottery winners, celebrities, or dot-com millionaires, for example) and who squandered it until they had nothing left. The amount of your income will not determine the amount of your "family profit" unless you manage it well. When you work together to handle your finances intelligently, you can create the financial security you need to live life comfortably. When your partnership extends to making smooth financial decisions and meeting your money goals without struggling and arguing, you'll find that everything else you do becomes less stressful.

Helen, forty-nine, and George, fifty-two, have been married six years. Both are widowed, so this is a second marriage for each of them. They have two children, Laurie, six, and Karen, twenty-three months, and Helen has one daughter, Bethany, nine, from her first marriage. George is a civilian working for the military, and Helen is a nurse. In their previous marriages, Helen and George had both followed traditional customs, with the man managing most of the money. Helen had often felt frustrated with this arrangement, and George felt burdened by all the responsibility. Each of them, of course, had to handle finances alone after their spouses died. Helen learned to manage her finances out of necessity and now feels very confident. So, when they began discuss living together, they talked about not wanting to repeat the patterns of their past marriages. By following the "Guidelines for Using Business

Skills at Home"(see below), they found it was much easier to discuss their options in a businesslike manner. Both of them agreed that their financial matters would be handled jointly and all money decisions would be made together. "I discovered, to my surprise," says George, "that I really didn't know how to share the decisions, so it was very awkward at first. I'm glad we began talking about it before we commingled our finances and our homes, because I had to learn to work together with Helen, and not just make the decisions myself."

"George had trouble listening to my opinions at first," Helen responds, "but after a few discussions, he began to realize that my ideas were helpful and sensible. Now we work things out together, and it's better for both of us. We have a considerable amount of assets between us, and we're working to leave a legacy to our children and grandchildren."

SOLUTION
Using Business Skills at Home

Viewing your family dispassionately as a business doesn't sound romantic, but if you can step back from your feelings long enough to view your relationship from this perspective, your financial situation makes more sense, money problems will be easier to solve, and you'll be able to discuss financial decisions with less difficulty.

Guidelines for Using Business Skills at Home

1. Don't react—respond: As I said in the previous chapter, neither of you would argue with the boss, colleagues at work, or a child's teacher the way you argue with each other. Even if your boss makes you angry, most likely you would use self-control at the office and blow off steam in private to your co-workers or a friend. Then, when you had a chance to think about the situation, you'd develop a better way of handling it and perhaps approach your boss with a thoughtful response.

You can do the same thing with your spouse when you have a money problem. Instead of saying the first thing that occurs to you, such as criticism or blaming, stop and think of a response more likely to lead to a discussion of the problem, rather than an argument.

2. Use positive manipulation: We often think of manipulation as a bad thing, as dishonest. However, acting in a way that makes it more likely to get a good response is not always deceitful or insidious. When you present an idea or solution, think about what your spouse would like about it, and lead with that. "Honey, you know that new car you've been wanting? I think I have a way for us to get it. We could take out some equity on the house to renovate the kitchen, we could get your new car, and the interest would be so much cheaper than a car loan." This is truthful and thoughtful, and it clearly shows the husband how both of their wants can be taken care of, so it's more likely to get a positive response.

3. Have a formal meeting: Just as you would in business, sit down for a real meeting about important financial issues. Don't expect to be able to discuss finances successfully while you're on the run, when it's late at night, or while watching TV. Instead, make a date for discussing finances and take the time to sit down together, with all the proper information, and discuss your needs, wants, and means. Follow a meeting method like Robert's Rules of Order, to keep the discussion on track. If a difficult problem arises, use the problem-solving skills at the end of this chapter.

4. Take finances seriously: Healthy businesses keep a close eye on the bottom line. In marriage, this means being careful about your money, but also not using money as a weapon against each other, or being irresponsible about it. A successful, happy marriage requires that both partners act like grownups. It's not surprising if you have disagreements about how much to save, when and what to spend, and who makes financial decisions, because such differences are normal between people.

If you take them seriously, and sit down to solve them together with mutual goodwill, your different points of view will become assets, not problems.

5. Check in regularly: As you do in business, have a brief check-in as frequently as possible. In the morning, or the night before, compare your daily schedules. Even if the things on your schedule don't really involve your spouse, mention them, so that each of you will know if you're facing anything important or challenging in the day ahead. When you have an idea of what's involved in each other's daily lives while you're apart, you will be much more able to respond in a helpful fashion to each other, especially when sudden changes or problems arise. For example, you can say, "I have to pick up some clients at the airport today, and I don't know what the traffic will be like, so I could be late tonight."

When you follow these guidelines for handling money together, you'll understand each other better, and you'll both understand your goals and feel more motivated to follow the plans you make.

STRUGGLE

Money Styles

Money is one of the biggest generators of problems, arguments, and resentment in long-term relationships. Couples argue about spending, saving, budgeting, and disparity in earnings. The traditional view of relationships assumes that all money should be pooled, but it isn't always that simple. If you both work, a difference in income can mean struggling about who pays for what, or whose income determines your lifestyle. If one of you works, and the other stays home to care for children, or perhaps go to school, the wage earner can resent paying the bills, and the homemaker can feel restricted and unappreciated. Different financial habits (one likes to save, the other spends more or doesn't keep track) can become a source of argument. For many couples, separating your money makes things run smoother; you don't wind up struggling for control. You can split expenses evenly, or work out a percentage share if your incomes are different. However you decide to do it, you need a clear, mutual understanding of your agreement.

SITUATION
Pool Finances or Not?

Establishing a level of financial independence from each other is usually the best way to mitigate any issues that can arise. But, whether you pool funds or separate them, communication, goal setting, and teamwork are the skills you and your spouse need to develop if you are to manage your checkbook and relationship.

> "In many ways," says Dorothy, "Bill and I seem to be opposites. I was attracted to his self-confidence and style, but sometimes his attitude makes me anxious."
>
> "I have always loved Dorothy's down-to-earth style, and her warmth," Bill acknowledges, "But her practical nature and my desire to show off can clash."

It is quite common to be drawn to someone with a different style, but those differences can create clashes when it comes to handling your money. Frequently, when I counsel couples, I find that having some separate funds minimizes the struggle about how to handle money.

Having money that you manage by yourself, in addition to the joint finances, gives each of you some room to express your personality differences. Yes, one of you might save more and the other spend more, but if you work out your division of funds sensibly, you'll cover the basics in your joint funds, which feels like teamwork, and have some leeway in your individual funds, which feels like freedom. If you're both competitive, think how great it could be if you began competing in investing your personal funds—that could be a race to riches! The key to separating some funds is to reach an agreement about how much of your total income needs to be kept jointly, to cover household expenses, savings, investments, and large purchases, and how much you can afford to have as discretionary cash.

Separating your checkbooks or credit or debit cards is one solution that often works well. For example, you can have a checkbook or debit card for each partner and a common checkbook, debit, or credit card for paying major bills like mortgages, utilities, household and child expenses, and groceries. If you have credit cards, the individual ones must stay within your individual budget for discretionary funds and be paid off each month. If you decide to buy a household item or car on credit, that would be handled through the joint funds. When you have a joint checkbook, credit card, or debit card, you have a way for both of you to be aware of your financial situation, including your individual and joint funds, on a regular basis, even if only one of you keeps the records. If only one of you is the wage earner, even temporarily, you need a clear agreement about how much income is at the disposal of the non-earner. Many couples who begin keeping their funds mostly separate decide to pool everything after a number of years, as the trust builds between them.

SOLUTION
Money Talks

You can avoid many misunderstandings and arguments by having regular discussions about finances, big and small. By adding money discussions to your regularly scheduled weekly meetings, you can keep current and avoid confusion and anxiety about how you're doing. Regular money talks will also enhance your feeling of partnership and keep you on track with savings, investments, and plans for the future. Bills, social planning, long-term goals, and working on your relationship are just some of the issues you'll discuss. Just sitting down once a week to talk about what happened and bringing the checkbook up to date can be a good management tool—and a time to talk about long-term plans such as purchasing a house or paying off college debt. Use the time not only to take stock of your finances, but of your relationship, too. Ask each other what is going well and what needs improvement.

The following guidelines will help you maintain an atmosphere of cooperation and teamwork, planning and problem solving in the businesslike manner described above. You can turn this weekly meeting into something that you look forward to, not an ordeal that you dread. As you talk about positive solutions and setting out long-term goals, many financial problems will be solved as they arise, while they are small and before they become difficult. If you share the time and energy in a mutually beneficial way, it can become a social occasion. Make it a pleasant opportunity; go out to dinner together or wait until the children are asleep or have a late breakfast on a Saturday morning. Use the following guidelines to help you.

Guidelines for Money Discussions
1. Share your different attitudes about money. Talk about how your families dealt with money, and what you liked and didn't like about their style. Share your observations about how

various friends handle money, and share what you think. Then make the discussion more personal by talking about how you feel about money, spending, saving, and your future dreams.

Dorothy and Bill couldn't seem to stop fighting over money. He loves to spend it, she wants to save it. They're relatively well off, but she still gets nervous when they take money out of savings for purchases or put items on credit cards. Her husband says they should live in the moment. After numerous arguments and mutual accusations, they sought counseling because they were afraid that their money problems would ruin their marriage. I advised them to use these guidelines because learning to cooperate about their finances was crucial to their future success as a couple, so they decided to begin discussing their dreams and hopes for their future. Dorothy and her husband need to talk, to begin with. They began to listen to each other's feelings about money. And they understood, for the first time, how their attitudes stemmed from different childhood experiences. Bill could understand that Dorothy's parents were poor but proud, and he admired her strong family ties and thriftiness. Dorothy was able to empathize because Bill often felt deprived at school if he didn't have the clothes or gear the other students had, or what he saw on TV. She understood that while Bill's family was also poor, they were not as close, and they spent rather than saved. As Dorothy and Bill came to understand each other's feelings and background, their money differences made more sense. They decided to work together to make the most of their differences. Bill could learn from Dorothy's thrift, and Dorothy could learn to relax a bit and enjoy money more.

2. Discuss long-term joint financial goals (such as a new home, baby, etc.). The previous guideline should lead you naturally into further discussion of your long-term goals and specific steps you need to follow to reach them. Steps should include saving and/or raising money to realize your goals and a plan for how long you think it will take.

Once Dorothy and Bill reached a more mutual understanding, they decided to develop a plan to save money for their future goals: to buy a house bigger than the condo they lived in now, with room for a family.

3. Put your plan to work. Once you have the steps outlined, break the first couple of steps down into small increments and choose steps for which each of you will take the responsibility in the coming week.

Dorothy and Bill each agreed to do some research into the local real estate market and financing to decide how much of a down payment they would need to have saved, and how much equity they had in their condo. Dorothy called some realtors, and read the real estate classified ads, and Bill called banks and finance companies to inquire about loan rates and down payments.

4. Establish separate checking accounts or personal spending budgets. As part of your plans, you may want to open separate checking accounts and savings accounts for building your dreams and agree on budgets for personal spending from your available funds. (See budgeting steps later in the chapter.)

They both recognized that Bill needed a little financial freedom, as a reward for working hard, and that Dorothy felt good about saving, so they decided on separate portions of their joint income for each to spend, and Dorothy volunteered to save and invest some of their monthly income. Bill promised to stay within his spending limit and to discuss with Dorothy before buying anything that cost over an agreed-on maximum. They agreed on a monthly amount to save, and to invest. Dorothy agreed to keep Bill informed of how she was investing their money, and how the investments were doing.

5. Discuss how the plan is going on a weekly basis. Keep this discussion going every week, and keep each other informed about how your plans are going. This is a good time to discuss the bills that need to be paid, changes in income or expenses, and what you need to do to accommodate the changes.

> Dorothy and Bill checked in weekly, to discuss how the agreement was going. When Bill got a raise, and had stayed within his spending limit, they agreed to add some of the extra money to his personal cash, and the rest would go into savings and investment. Dorothy not only was managing the joint finances well, she had saved some money from her personal funds. They were ahead of their goals, so Bill suggested they use some of the extra to take a little weekend vacation to a favorite place of Dorothy's (which delighted her).

6. Keep talking. No matter how well or poorly your finances are going at any given time; keep your financial discussions going. The more frequently you discuss your finances, the less difficult the discussions will be, and the more likely that you'll make good financial choices.

Money doesn't have to be a wedge between you and your partner. It can be a great tool for learning more about one another. Money doesn't make happiness, but using money matters as a discussion point can help your relationship grow. Making long-term plans, helping reach goals, and improving your quality of life are just some of the things you will be able to accomplish—together. Bill and Dorothy were so relieved that their money situation seemed solved that they stopped having their weekly meetings, and suddenly they found they were arguing again. As soon as they resumed the meetings, the arguing stopped.

Planning vs. Spontaneity

Only after Dorothy and Bill began to communicate with each other were they able to reach a mutual agreement. When Bill was reassured that he'd have some money to spend, and Dorothy was able to save and invest, they both relaxed. The rules weren't so strict that Bill couldn't follow them, and the financial confusion that made Dorothy anxious was gone. Their deal that the savings and any expenditure over a certain amount would be discussed made it possible for them to feel relaxed and generous with each other again. The weekly meetings allowed each of them to feel that everything was under control.

But what if your partner's spending is dangerous or borderline? What if one of you is likely to spend the rent money if you're not watched? If things are that bad, you have an issue for therapy. Spending money can be an addiction. Or maybe there's a drug, phone sex, or gambling problem. That would require drastic measures, and one of you may have to control all the money (have a spouse's paycheck deposited automatically to an account only you sign on, and dole out a reasonable allowance). If your spouse is spending way too much money, a confrontation is in order. Say "I love you, and I want to be married to you, but I'm worried about our finances. Please come with me to therapy so we can work it out." If your partner says "I know I've got a problem, and I agree we need to do something about it. I'm willing to go to therapy with you," that's a good response, so don't delay, and use the "Guidelines for Finding and Using Therapy Wisely" in chapter 9. The therapist will probably suggest a twelve-step program for your spouse and make some recommendations about controlling the money until your spouse has the problem under control. If, on the other hand, your spouse is lying about the problem, or refuses to admit it's a problem, despite the evidence of credit card bills, missing cash, and so on, you'll have to take matters into your own hands.

If you can find a way to control the finances, including your spouse's income, dole out small amounts of cash as needed, and cancel the credit cards, do so. If you are not able to do that, then go for counseling to learn how. Your therapist may suggest a nonaddicted spouse's twelve-step program or financial counseling for you.

SITUATION
Different Attitudes Lead to Stalemate

Most of the time, the problem is not that severe, and it's simply a matter of differences in attitudes and beliefs. Because you see the situation from your different perspectives, you get locked into fights about who's right and who's wrong, which can become emotional. As we explored earlier in this chapter, using a more businesslike style can keep your discussions from getting emotional and defensive. The following guidelines for problem solving will help you reach agreement when you are struggling. While they are somewhat similar to the previous guidelines for discussion, the focus here is on getting past a problem, rather than discussing your general situation.

SOLUTION
Problem Solving

These guidelines will help you to break free of your stalemate, bypass the arguments, and move on to productive discussion.

Guidelines for Problem Solving

1. Get started: Get started by congratulating each other on how far you've come since the beginning of your relationship, on how well you've solved some past problems, and how well you feel you work together. (Or how much you'd like to begin working together better.)

2. Describe the problem: Begin by discussing your dreams and your wants, as you do in the regular discussions, and then move to discussing problems. Spend only as much time on the problems as you need to be sure both of you understand what they are, and then switch to discussing possible solutions. Don't get caught in the trap of talking about the problems over and over, because it leads to frustration and bickering.

3. Brainstorm: To free yourselves up from limited thinking, try brainstorming—make a lot of suggestions, even if they're silly or outrageous, and don't criticize them or respond with why they won't work. If you can laugh a little at your financial problems, you'll find them easier to handle, and if you both have permission to mention all the ideas you have, outrageous or serious, it will free up and encourage creative thinking. Don't try to make a decision at this stage, just record all the ideas.

4. Evaluate the options: Once you think you have enough ideas, move to the decision stage. The rule here is: "I want you and me to both get what we want." Make it clear to each other that it's not a contest, and you're going to work together to find a solution that works for both of you. Look at suggestions you made, one by one, and evaluate each one for practicality (Can we afford it? Will it solve the problem? Is it logical?) and whether it solves the problem and also satisfies both of your wants.

5. Experiment and research: If you can't come up with an option that works, it usually means neither of you knows enough about the subject, and you need more information. Agree to do some research—ask an expert, take a class, look up info on the Internet, or try one of the options as an experiment, to see if it will work, without committing to it. For example:

- If you're thinking about changing jobs to make more income or have more time at home, research what jobs are out there before leaving your current situation.

When you find something you think will work, try the commute, talk to people who work there, and run the numbers on the new salary, to see what it does to your budget. Or,

- If you've been a stay-at-home mom and you want to go back to work, take a temporary job for a couple of months to see how it feels and how it changes your family life.

- If you think you'd like to live in a different city or state, spend some extended vacation time there; check out the schools, the housing market, the salaries, and recreation activities there. Attend some community events to see how you like the people you'll be living with.

Once you've done the research or tried the change on, you'll have a lot better idea of which solution will work for both of you.

6. Make an agreement: When you've found a solution that suits both of you and solves the problem, the only other thing you need to do is state your agreement out loud, to make sure you're both clear and understand it the same way. When this kind of problem solving is new to you, it often helps to write down what you've decided. Then, if confusion arises in the future, you can go back to the written agreement for clarity. Keep in mind that any decision can be renegotiated, so if your circumstances or preferences change later, you can just follow this process again.

Budgeting and Savings

Your marital finances (as we discussed earlier in this chapter) are similar to a business in which the two of you are partners. Every successful business has a financial plan, whether formal or informal. The financial plan in your marriage is called a budget. Budgeting, like dieting, is one of those actions many men and women have good intentions about but don't seem to accomplish. The good news is that when you know how to do it, budgeting is much easier than dieting.

A budget, of course, begins with income and assets (which is the net worth of all your possessions, investments, and savings).

Savings

Savings are more than just a financial asset. Having savings gives you a safety net, security, and much more flexibility than you would have otherwise. When you have savings, you aren't devastated each time there's a financial setback, such as a medical expense, or a car or home repair problem. Savings also represent the power to make your dreams come true. Yes, it's possible to take that vacation or buy new furniture on credit, but if you have the savings to do it, you'll pay a lot less. Interest charges for credit, over time, can cost two to three times the amount you're borrowing. Savings can create a down payment for your "dream home" or prepare in advance for all the extra expenses of having children. One of the easiest ways to develop savings so you can invest and build capital to fund your dreams is to "pay yourself first" which means to set aside a percentage (10 percent or more) of your income and put it in savings before you pay any bills or spend anything. Don't wait until all the bills are paid to set aside savings. Set aside at least a small amount first, and then pay the bills as you can. Even if this pinches your free spending money at first, you'll soon grow used to living on your available income, and your savings account will grow at an amazing rate. As you get increases in income, such as a raise, try putting the raise into savings, along with the percentage you're putting aside already. If you like, you can celebrate using the raise the first time it appears on your paycheck (this will also give you a chance to see how much it is after taxes), then put it into savings from then on. If you have the opportunity, have the money directly deposited into your savings plan. The money to invest, buy your dream home, or get your new baby off to a great start will grow quickly and relatively painlessly.

The following steps will make it easy for you to learn to budget and maximize your financial power.

How to Budget
Step 1. Know Your Income
A good budget begins with knowing your personal financial picture.

Write down everything you earn. If you get a salary, this is quite simple—just record your net pay. If you have several sources of money, such as child support, extra jobs, gifts from family, or a small business, knowing your income can be more difficult. To find out what it is, you may have to keep track of all the money you receive by writing it down. If your income varies from month to month, keep track of it for several months and then take an average (add together all your income for six months and divide by six to get an average per month).

Step 2. Know Your Expenses
Once you know how much money you take in, you need to know how you spend it. Keeping a record is the best way to do this.

1. Write down your fixed bills. These include rent, utilities (gas, electricity, water, trash pick-up), car payment, school fees (yours or your child's), insurance payments, real estate and income taxes (these are usually paid yearly, so divide by twelve), and loan payments. When you're done, you should have a list of all your fixed expenses—those bills you must pay every month. This is easier to do if you pay bills by check or have a computer accounting system, but you can do it just by keeping track of receipts, also.

2. Write down the rest of your expenses. These will vary with the time of year and the decisions you make about clothing, food, entertainment, personal-care items like soap and toothpaste, holiday and vacation expenses, repairs and maintenance, and so on. This category is a lot more variable than the fixed expenses, and these expenses are usually where you can manage to create more room in the budget by cutting back.

3. Analyze your expenses. One of the best ways to track both variable and fixed expenses is to pay everything by check, debit card, or online and then analyze your checkbook or online statement after a couple of months. In your record of the checks you've written, you'll have a listing of much of what you spent. If you frequently spend cash, bring home receipts and write down all your cash expenditures for at least two months in a small notebook or expenses journal. If you use a credit card to buy gasoline or other items, don't forget to include your credit card purchases and payments, too.

4. Total your income and expenses by month. Then subtract the total expenses for each month from the total income for that month. Hopefully, you'll come up with more income than expenses, but for many couples this figure turns out to be a negative number. If that's true, it means you're sliding into debt more every month.

Keeping track of your income and expenses, learning what you spend money on and how much of your income you spend may be an eye-opener, but you'll find it is worthwhile to know where you stand. If you are earning more than you're spending, good for you! You can put aside some of the surplus for saving and investing. If you're spending more than you're earning, you have to make some decisions. You can find ways to increase your income or you can spend less. Go back to your original list of expenses and see what you can leave out, or go back to your income and see whether there's any way you can increase it.

Once you know whether you're spending more than you're earning, or vice versa, you're ready to set up a budget.

Step 3. Set Up a Budget

Using your current spending as a guide, analyze what you are spending for each item—food, clothing, entertainment, transportation or auto expense, fixed expenditures such as rent, and so on. Make a list of each category of expense and decide on an amount to spend each month on that item. Some people make this list on paper, while others use file cards or a computer. Home computer programs such as Quickbooks have forms you can fill out to do this. If you pay for things by credit or debit card, use your statements to see what you've been spending for the last few months.

When Daisy and Mike reviewed their spending, Daisy said, "I guess you're right, Mike, We do spend too much money on things we don't need and eating out. We're not saving enough to help the children with their education, and that's important to me."

Mike suggested, "Why don't we deposit both our paychecks, and immediately put 10 percent into savings. Then we'd know we're not going to spend everything."

Daisy agreed. Together, they reviewed every expense, beginning with necessities, like groceries, mortgage, medical insurance, and utilities. Once this was done, they knew how much they had to spend on variable expenses such as entertainment, school expenses, groceries, and haircuts and clothing for both parents and children. They discussed how much they'd been spending for each category, and set limits for how much to spend each month on each item, based on their available funds.

Daisy was better with numbers and records, so they agreed she'd keep track of expenses on the computer from their receipts, and if they went over budget on any item, such as school clothes, they either reduced the amount they'd spend on entertainment that month or they'd take the surplus out of the next month's budget for school clothes. Mike said, "But let's not allow ourselves to dip into next month's budget unless there's a reason we both agree on, and let's not let that go more than one month." Any time they didn't use the whole budget for a particular month, the surplus increased the budget for that category the following month. For example, if the children didn't need their school-expense money in the summer, by fall they had enough to go to the store and stock up on supplies just before school began. Or, if they didn't spend everything in the entertainment category, they could add the extra to their vacation allowance.

Daisy says, "Once we developed the budget and stuck to it for a few months, our arguments about money subsided. We stopped fussing and blaming each other because the numbers were clear, factual, and impartial. It even helped keep the kids from begging for outrageously priced running shoes or cell phones, because they could see by the numbers that if they spend $100 on shoes, they had almost nothing to spend on other clothes. I loved the teaching tool the budget became for the kids. Now, when they want something, I can say 'Let's look at the budget and see if it will work.' I have to admit it works on me, too. Now, if one of us can't have something, it's the budget that's the bad guy, and not Mike or me." Mike says, "This budget thing and our savings are going so well that with my next union contract increase, we're going to increase savings and eventually buy a bigger house."

Budgeting can be valuable even if you're in better financial condition than Daisy and Mike were.

Dorothy and Bill had enough money, but when they followed the same process that Daisy and Mike used, they quickly learned the importance of knowing how much they were spending on each expense and what was left over after savings and fixed expenses. Dorothy began the process by saying, "Bill, let's sit down with our income statements and our credit and debit card statements and make a budget. It's a great way for us to see how much we really have to spend, and to plan for buying a bigger home or running our own business someday." Bill agreed—he was the one who wanted the business and the home, so that was great incentive for him. He was used to doing computer spreadsheets for his work, so that's how they decided to work the numbers. They put their combined income into the spreadsheet, just as Bill recorded his sales at work, and then they entered their expenses (they averaged a few months credit and debit card statements to come up with a one-month average) just as Bill entered his expenses at work. The spreadsheet program automatically did the math for them.

Once they had a good budget they could plan ahead for improvements to their home and for investments to get the most out of their money. "Because we had a budget and Bill kept all his agreements and stayed within the bounds," says Dorothy, "I felt much more secure about his spending, and I realized, although his style was different from mine, he understood about setting limits and he did value savings and investments. Budgeting made me feel much more secure about our future."

Bill said, "Seeing the numbers in black and white made things clearer for me. Instead of thinking that Dorothy was just being scared or stingy, I can see how much I'm spending, and she's spending, and we have clear goals. It's worth it to me to skip the new suit or upgrading the car if I know we're going to be able to take a great vacation in the short term, or in the future, buy a nicer home and start a business of our own."

However you decide to set up your budget (you may want to take a class or get some advice from a CPA, a certified financial planner, or a friend if the instructions above are not enough for you), plan how much of your income you'll spend on each expense and stick to it. The point of budgeting is to live within your means and provide for savings. No matter how much or how little income you have, planning and using your money wisely will ultimately help you reach your goals, and the combination of calm discussion and living within a budget will resolve most of your disagreements about finances.

Chapter 3

SOLVING SEX SQUABBLES

No matter what you see in the movies, or how the locker room or girlfriend talk sounds, maintaining a long-term sexual relationship is not easy. Because most of us are very vulnerable and at our most insecure when it comes to sexual issues, sexual trust is among the most difficult type of trust to build. During sex, feelings of attractiveness, loveableness, and self-esteem are exposed and challenged, and a thoughtless remark or action can set off powerful emotions.

Fighting about sex, or using sex as punishment, can create devastating and lasting damage to your marriage. Without healthy intimacy and a good sexual connection, your relationship is at risk to outside temptation. Let's explore some of the biggest problems in sex and intimacy. It has long been known that partners who engage each other in arguing can maintain a strong intimate bond as long as their arguments aren't too damaging or violent. The important thing is that they communicate during their arguments and make up warmly afterward. Coldness and withdrawal, on the other hand, make it almost impossible for a couple to bond.

Whether a marriage is blissful or painful depends not only on how spouses handle the inevitable conflicts that arise, but also on how they respond to opportunities for emotional intimacy, researchers found.

STRUGGLE
Withdrawal

There are three distinct ways couples can withdraw from intimacy: angry withdrawal, conflict avoidance, and intimacy avoidance. When a partner withdraws and becomes unresponsive, even though no anger is openly expressed, the survival of the relationship can be threatened as severely as in a partnership of constant fighting and negativity.

One of the most common reasons couples fight about sex is that one or both of the partners feels rejected. What most people don't know is that it's very easy to withdraw from each other over the course of married life, and not so easy to come back together again.

Jan and Ron, former high school sweethearts, married right after graduation, fifteen years ago. They have two children. Jan works as a teacher's aide, and Ron is a building contractor, and their lives are very busy. The first several years of their marriage were happy, but lately, they've been bickering, and their sex life is nearly nonexistent. What can they do to re-establish the good feelings they used to have for each other?

"Sex was so easy when we first met." Ron says, "Now, we hardly get together at all. What happened to wanting to have sex? If I try to get close, she's never interested, and then we argue."

"I can't relax and enjoy sex when we never talk to each other," says Jan. "Ron comes home late from work, tired and cranky, we eat dinner while watching TV, and then it's bedtime, and he wants sex. Well, it doesn't work that way for me. So when I say no, we fight, and lose even more sleep. It's a vicious cycle."

SITUATION

Rejection and Disappointment Create Withdrawal

Withdrawal from interaction with your partner, especially when the appropriate response would be emotional closeness, warmth, and caring, can be fatal to your relationship. Withdrawing from intimate interaction begins with disappointment because unrealistic expectations about sex aren't met, and then solidifies into resentment. Once resentment, hurt feelings, and fear of rejection set in, sex becomes impossible.

> Like every couple, when Jan and Ron were dating, they had built-in transitions from alone time, work, or chores. Shaving and showering, getting dressed up, driving to meet, preparing for the date—these are all transitions, forms of pre-foreplay, which get you in the mood. You spend that time in pleasant anticipation. Now that they live together that anticipation has disappeared. Getting alone is what they must prepare for—not getting together.

Like Jan and Ron, you and your partner may have reached an impasse when it comes to sex, so that you connect by fighting instead of becoming intimate. Why does this happen, and what do you need to do to fix it?

A big part of the problem is unrealistic expectations influenced by media images. In romances in the movies and on TV, sex just happens. Eyes lock, breathing deepens, the background music swells, and the gorgeous stars are in a clinch. But it doesn't happen that way in busy married life.

Consider all the different attitudes and activities you share in a given day. You are workers, friends, troubleshooters, parents (to children or to each other), repairpersons, bill-payers, meal-makers, and many other things.

You can feel tired, exhilarated, defeated, successful, sexy, scared, vulnerable, angry, loving, indifferent, exhausted, and a host of other emotions. Most of the time, you and your partner are probably reacting to different stimuli in separate situations, bombarded by different ideas. One of you may be feeling triumphant (success at work; your child got an A) while the other is frustrated (the plumbing project isn't going well; your sister is being difficult). Only on a relaxed day, doing things together, are you likely to be in the kind of similar, complementary moods that lead to feeling intimate and sexy. Few of us have enough such relaxed days. As a result, the attraction and energy that seemed inexhaustible when you were first together may feel like it's fading away.

So, once your sex life has developed a problem like this, how do you fix it and end the conflict? How do you get compatible moods going?

SOLUTION
Develop Transitions and Increase Intimacy

How do you move from emptying the garbage to feeling romantic? By learning to create transitions. Think of a transition as a little preparation ritual that leads you into similar frames of mind by focusing both of you on each other. Don't expect the mutuality to "just be there" or to happen instantly. Remember to suggest or invite rather than complain or demand: You can say, "I'd love to spend a little time with you tonight, would you like to?"

Creating Intimacy

While enjoyable sex is an important part of marital life, creating a strong bond is the most reliable way to safeguard your connection. Fighting happens more often in marriages in which the intimacy and bonding aren't working. Intimacy is the art of making your partner feel understood and accepted.

When this feeling is created, barriers fall. Gentle touch, eye contact, a gentle sense of humor, and the right words all create the atmosphere. Commenting on your partner's looks or the day's activities positively will also help. To reconnect, be sure you are listening to each other and understanding your partner's needs and wants. The most powerful thing you can do to keep a marriage strong is form a partnership, a team, where both parties feel respected, cared about, and needed. If you really want to restore the marriage, begin not by complaining about your needs that aren't being met but by focusing on your mate's needs. Once your good connection is restored, you can begin to work out the issues.

Here are some ways to bring intimacy back:

Guidelines for Increasing Intimacy

1. Make recreation, play, and fun a priority. Put more energy into making your partner laugh, and you'll find a playful approach will motivate both you and your spouse to want to be close. Pleasure, humor, leisure activities, and silliness are ways we recharge, renew our energy, restore our hope and positive outlook, and connect with each other. Don't allow too much of your time to be absorbed by TV, e-mail, computer games, or other people who are not important.

2. Don't let your expectations get out of line. Fun and intimacy do not depend on spending money or going to extremes; they don't depend on a particular setting or activity, and they don't have to take a lot of time. Enjoying yourselves is an internal process. You can be close sitting still and talking about interesting or enjoyable things, working together in your garden, playing with the kids or the dog, or doing a puzzle. Singing, dancing, playing a sport or a board game may be what you need to feel close. Through play we reconnect with our heart, our childlike self, and the intuitive, spontaneous responses that lead to sexual connections.

Jan says, "It's not attractive to me when Ron and I don't spend any time together. When I finally got him to hear that we needed to spend time together, he agreed to cut down his time on the computer at home and be with me at least some evenings a week. That makes me feel a lot closer to him."

Yes, you can create intimacy with special occasions, something that requires a bit of advance planning; but when you look back on your most intimate experiences, they are more likely to have been spontaneous and simple rather than elaborate and expensive.

3. Develop "signals" that work. A special light in the bedroom (when it's lit, at least one of you is interested) bringing home flowers, dressing up, a certain touch or phrase.

Jan and Ron realized that part of the reason they were struggling is that they didn't know how or when to initiate sex, or who was responsible for beginning. After some discussion, they decided that the phrase "can we cuddle?" would be their catchphrase and that they'd agree to spend a little time in the evening before bed snuggled together on the couch. This gave them both a chance to relax and feel connected, and sex often naturally followed. Jan says, "This solved the whole problem for me. I get to be the one who asks to cuddle sometimes, and I get a chance to feel close to Ron before sex." "It works for me, too," says Ron. "I know I'm not going to get rejected when I suggest cuddling, and it's pretty easy to move from snuggling to sex, so most of the time I get what I want, and if sometimes I don't, it's OK; because I know next time I'll probably succeed."

Be careful that your desire for intimacy is always a request and not a demand. The difference is that a request can take "no" for an answer. A demand is oppressive; a request is complementary. Demands push you apart; requests invite the other person to come closer.

Once you have established some transitions that work, try some surprises. A surprise means you haven't consulted each other, so as with all surprises, give your partner time to respond and be prepared to change the details if necessary. You could be showered, scented, and dressed in something you know your mate will like when he or she comes home from work, and make your move. Observe your mate's response, and be prepared to back off if you've picked a bad time. Your sense of humor works well here. When they work well, surprises can add some excitement and energy to your sexual relationship; but only if done infrequently.

4. Make reservations at a romantic spot. Give them to your lover inside a sexy or romantic card during a quiet dinner out. Because it's a surprise, build some flexibility into the plan, and make sure the plans would feel good to your partner, not just to you.

5. Sex is a physical form of communication, and it requires some time. Give yourselves transition time before getting sexual. Don't expect to be able to jump into bed and "get it on." Allow time for quiet conversation and sensual touch. A "quickie" can be lots of fun, but the fun disappears if it becomes your only option.

For most of us, "romance" is important to some degree in encouraging a sexual mood. The relaxed anticipation produced by the right music, soft lights, and sweet words makes an ideal atmosphere for intimacy, which leads to verbal and physical affection. Keep in mind that what feels romantic or sexy differs for men and women, so include cues that work for both of you. Many couples find that watching erotic or romantic movies helps set the mood.

Intimacy is only possible when there is also sufficient personal space. Allow a little distance, regularly. "How can I miss you if you don't go away?" is a humorous way to put it. You need some separate activities, friends, and interests to keep your desire for each other fresh. It's great for your relationship when you have something interesting to tell your spouse about when you come home.

6. Don't let romance slide. Don't forget to bring home flowers, send cards, create or buy silly little gifts for each other. Write poetry, silly notes or songs, clip a magazine cartoon, or simply speak the positive things you feel. Take an extra few minutes to set a scene when you have quiet time together, set the table a little nicer when you're home alone for dinner. If you know your spouse finds some aspect of a movie sexy or romantic, copy it. Bring your wife the same kind of flowers, or show up in the bedroom in a similar slip to the one your husband admired on the lead actress. If the romantic couple in the movie takes a long, romantic walk in the woods, try walking together in a local park.

7. Revisit memories of your early days together. Visit places that have meaning to you: the restaurant where you had your first date, the park where you met, the romantic hideaway spot where you camped out. Play your favorite love songs; rent an old, romantic movie and eat popcorn; do a crossword puzzle; go golfing; cook your favorite foods together. Reliving your early dates can rekindle the early feelings.

Culturally, women have more permission for romance than men do, but it has been said many times that men are the true romantics. Many romantic poems, song lyrics, movies, and plays are written by men. Don't worry about your "image"; be willing to risk feeling a little silly from time to time. It's a great tonic for your relationship. Men, the major reward for you is more and better sex. Women, your reward is feeling loved and desired. You'll both have a great time, and enjoy it.

STRUGGLE
Satisfaction and Frequency

Ah, sex: To be, or not to be, when, and how much—that is the question. People have different sexual needs, wants, styles, and frequencies, so it's no surprise that couples frequently argue about frequency and satisfaction. What usually happens is that one partner wants sex more often than the other (contrary to popular belief, the man isn't always the most eager; in some couples it's the woman). The partner who has less drive feels somewhat threatened by his or her spouse's approaches for sex, and refuses, without discussion and usually with an excuse: I'm too tired, I have a headache, I have to get up early. Because they don't understand or discuss the difference in their sex drives, the approaching spouse feels rejected. A rejected spouse will usually try for a while, but without honest talk, the situation usually gets worse. A couple's disagreement about sexual frequency may lead to giving one another the "silent treatment," or quarrels about "you don't love me"—which is another way to avoid talking directly about the problem.

SITUATION
Different Sexual Needs

If your partner wants to have sex when you don't, it's natural for him or her to be disappointed. But if your partner pressures you and gets angry, hurt, or hostile when you say no, that can cause a fight that will only push you further away. On the other hand, if there's not much warmth or sexual energy at all, it's important to wonder why. Sex is a vital part of a lasting relationship. It takes some effort to keep a sexual relationship satisfying over the long haul, even if you begin with a solid sexual connection. If, after marriage, you don't seem to be compatible sexually, or your ideas about appropriate sexuality and frequency are at odds, those differences can become a big problem in maintaining your long-term relationship.

> Cheryl and Dirk have been in an affectionate but sexless relationship for six months, so it's not surprising that Cheryl is worried. She wonders, "Is this inevitable in marriage? Is it true that if you put a penny in a jar every time you have sex during the first year, and take a penny out every time after that, the jar will never be empty? It seems that the only people having nookie in long-term relationships are those who have tension and anger simmering beneath the surface or see each other so infrequently that they feel the need to bump and grind when they reunite."
>
> Dirk says, "I like sex as much as the next guy, but Cheryl is always at me. She wants to have sex, which would be great, but then it has to be romantic sex. She wants lights, music, enough foreplay, and if I touch her too rough, or too slow, or in the wrong place, she complains. She wants an orgasm every time, but she often takes a long time. I get too frustrated, I can't keep my sexual energy going, and now I don't want to even try. But, I also don't want to be trapped in a situation that becomes less exciting with each passing year. But, I can't tell her she's too demanding. She'll just get mad at me, and we'll be in the same boat, only worse."

The folk legend about the penny in the jar that Cheryl relates illustrates a belief many couples have: Once you're in a committed relationship, the romance and passion quickly fade. As we discussed above, when you commit to your relationship and live together for an extended period of time, and get more comfortable and familiar with each other, the initial excitement and newness eventually wears off, and the passion can lessen because you begin to get into a familiar day-to-day routine. The conditions that made sex effortless have changed. In addition to that, our expectations of "zipless" sex, the concept Erica Jong created in her novel, *Fear of Flying*, to identify effortless, irresistible sexual connection, makes us much more critical of the small differences and disappointments that routinely happen when two people attempt to connect. These high expectations are what Dirk is talking about. He feels overwhelmed and defeated by Cheryl's demands and criticism.

You'll be glad to know lack of sex is not inevitable in long-term relationships by any means. Less frequency, less intensity, and less creativity are all fairly common experiences, but no sex at all is not a given. Cheryl is right in that some couples need to argue and have "make-up sex" to get their juices flowing, and that frequent absences do increase lust for many couples. But if both you and your partner are in good physical and mental health, with no major pains or depression, then there is no reason you shouldn't be feeling sexual toward each other. If you once had a satisfactory sexual connection and now you don't, it indicates that there's a problem you need to solve.

SOLUTION
Developing Trust

Dirk and Cheryl need to share the truth about what's hampering their sex to solve their problem and get back to enjoying each other. If you and your partner are struggling because one of you wants more sex than the other does, or one of you is dissatisfied or feels rejected, it's vital that you learn how to talk about the problem without creating arguments and hurt feelings.

Sex Discussions

Not telling your partner the truth about your sexual feelings and discomfort is actually another form of withholding. To have a successful sexual relationship, it's crucial to be honest, and to hear the truth without overreacting, blaming, or punishing your lover for telling it. Sexual trust is one of the most difficult kinds of trust to build because most of us are very vulnerable and at our most insecure about sexual issues. Here are some steps to help you.

To begin to solve sexual problems, you need to find a way to begin talking. Set aside some time for talking to build trust.

1. Guarantee gentleness: Begin by guaranteeing each other mutual gentleness; don't move to the other steps until both of you can agree that if you get upset, hurt, anxious, or angry, you'll take three deep breaths and calm down before answering. Stating what you want or feel instead of accusing each other will make it easier to be heard. Try using "I" messages—speak in terms of yourself, what you feel or want, such as:

- "I want the house to be clean."
- "I don't like what you did."
- "I feel hurt and criticized."

Rather than

- "You make a mess."
- "You did it wrong."
- "You hurt me."

This will cause each of you to take responsibility for your own feelings, and it also makes it less likely that you'll get defensive and argue. If your discussion begins to turn into an argument or criticism, agree that you'll stop until you both calm down. Hold hands and stay close; it helps you stay calm and remember that you're partners. For the purposes of this discussion, each of you should be brief and stick with one thing at a time. Later, when you have practiced this way of communicating, your discussions will become easier and you'll be able to talk more freely.

2. Risk the truth: Invite your partner to risk telling you one small truth, which can be about anything: something he or she likes or doesn't like about sex; a fear about body image or performance; concerns about hygiene or grooming. Use "I" messages to state it.

3. Listen and understand: Listen carefully, and then take whatever time is necessary to be able to respond calmly. Take a few deep breaths if you are anxious or your feelings are hurt. Respond by repeating in your own words what your partner said, or ask for more explanation if you need it. Ask your partner for confirmation that you understood what he or she said.

4. Respond with care: Once you and your spouse agree that you understand, then use "I" messages to respond to what he or she said. Keep your focus on being understanding and creating solutions.

5. Share your truth: Then use "I" messages to share a truth yourself, and give your partner enough time to hear it and to react to it. After your partner has responded with the same focus on being calm, ask for feedback, and listen to his/her feelings about what you said.

If being honest about sex is new for you, this exercise will help you understand how to create sexual honesty. Sharing your true feelings without criticizing or reacting negatively will create safety and build the trust between you. After a few rounds of this exercise, and especially after doing the exercise several times over a few weeks or months, your confidence will grow. Once you've developed a loving atmosphere free of fear, the honesty comes much easier, and understanding each other's concerns can be reached quickly.

A great side effect of this is that your sexual encounters will benefit, too. This kind of deep, open trust provides a sense of security that's an ideal environment for relaxed, open, and free sexual expression. When you both know you can say whatever comes to mind without fear of a negative response, you open mental and emotional doors that lead to very deep connections.

Once you have learned how to talk about sex openly, and in a gentle manner, you'll have a much better understanding of your similarities and differences, your strengths and weaknesses. Then you can use the following guidelines to develop new agreements about sex, and to solve any problems your differences have created.

Guidelines for Creating a Sexual Agreement

1. Set up a problem-solving session: Once you've practiced creating trust and sexual openness, finding solutions is much easier. Begin with reassurance and goodwill, reminding each other of your love and of your desire that your sexual relationship be fulfilling for both of you. Underneath your anxiety, frustration, and struggle, each of you is longing for the other to care about what you want, and to understand you. If you have difficulty talking to each other about this, you can read these guidelines aloud and follow them step-by-step. This is a prime opportunity to improve all the communication in your relationship and get you out of being stuck. Remind each other, "I love you, I want our relationship to be good for both of us."

2. Share your wants, needs, and ideas: Be honest about your sexual needs. Your partner may feel more like you do about sex than you think; but you'll never know that unless you're willing to express your own feelings and listen to him or her. Being honest means not only telling the truth but also being willing to hear the truth from each other.

Making honesty OK is the key to achieving sexual understanding. The only attitude that works is this one: "I may not like what you tell me, I may have trouble hearing it, but I will still love you, and we will work together to come to an agreement that works."

3. Avoid using threats, coercion, or pressure to get what you want: Overly dramatic statements such as "You don't care what I want," "If you insist on that, I'll leave you," or "You don't love me, or you wouldn't want that" don't work. Threats, emotional blackmail, and dire predictions close down discussion, and they don't change behavior—they just send it underground.

4. Allow room for mistakes, confusion, and renegotiation: It is important that your contract allows for flexibility and allows room for growth in your relationship as time passes. I recommend that as part of the contract you and your partner set up regular communication meetings to talk about your contract and to review how it is working.

5. Write down your agreement: Once you've reached an agreement, writing it down helps. You'll be sure you both understand your agreement in the same way when you get it written down to your mutual satisfaction. You can do it ceremoniously, in fancy type or script, or you can scribble it on a piece of paper. Make it as simple or legal-sounding as you like. The important part is that you both agree with what's written.

If all this sounds to good to be true, I recommend that you give it a try before rejecting the ideas. Mutual healing, gentle honesty, and acceptance create an atmosphere where love can grow, as long as the mutual respect and openness between you is carefully nurtured.

STRUGGLE
Dishonesty, Jealousy, Temptation, and Trust

Arguments about dishonesty, jealousy, and infidelity are basically about trust. Do you trust each other? Have you done something to damage that trust? Have you been betrayed in the past and therefore have a difficult time trusting this partner? Trust is not easy to maintain, because it is quite easily damaged. Early in a relationship, both partners get to demonstrate their trustworthiness. If promises are kept and feelings are respected, the trust grows. If the partners experience roughly the same degree of trust, the relationship will thrive. If one partner is not trustworthy, the other will feel betrayed. However, it is also true that a partner can feel betrayed even if the other person did nothing wrong, especially if that partner has already been betrayed in a previous relationship.

Betrayal is a powerful emotional issue. When we trust someone with our feelings, we take the risk of being very painfully let down. It's amazing to me that most people seem to be more cautious entrusting others with their money than with their innermost feelings and self-esteem.

Allowing emotional trust to grow the same way we allow financial trust to grow makes more sense. Thinking about investment of trust the way we think about investment of money makes it easier to understand: When you first meet someone, no matter how pleasant the encounter, you're not likely to take your life savings out of the bank, hand it to them and say, "If you treat this responsibly, we can be friends." Trusting someone else with your financial resources takes a long time. After years of friendship, in which the other person has demonstrated responsibility with money, you might happily and confidently make a loan or a financial partnership with him or her.

Emotional investments should be just as cautious. Waiting to see whether this person you're excited about is worthy of your emotional investment makes a lot more sense, but most people aren't cautious when they become involved in relationships. People who have been betrayed often realize in hindsight that they trusted someone who wasn't trustworthy in the first place—setting themselves up for disappointment and hurt. Once you have been betrayed in love, it is much more difficult to trust a second time, and if you don't understand how trust is built and maintained, it seems difficult and mysterious to sort it out. Often, innocent actions can threaten the trust in a relationship, as with Kim and James.

> When Kim met Rick through her work as a pharmaceutical representative, they hit it off immediately. They'd go to business seminars and dine together, but nothing more. Soon thereafter, she met and married James, and started having children. She met Rick occasionally for lunch, feeling as attracted as ever.
>
> "For a time, thinking of him and the lunch we shared was the highlight of my day, rather, my entire week, until I saw him the following week for lunch again," says Kim, age forty-one. James began to notice how I reacted, and got jealous. He wanted me to stop visiting Rick as a client and having lunch with him. I felt accused of doing something wrong, and I got defensive, so we fought a lot."

SITUATION
Secrecy, Fantasy, and Denial

> Kim didn't tell James of her infatuation with Rick and never explained that she wasn't acting on it, but James picked up the "vibes" and believed Kim was cheating or at least considering it. Kim felt his lack of trust and became hurt and defensive.

It's a very familiar story, one I work with repeatedly while counseling couples. Dishonesty and mistrust in relationships is a timeless problem, going back as far as history is recorded. The Bible and ancient Chinese, Greek, and Roman writings are full of stories of betrayed trust. Shakespeare wrote about it. *Othello* is about murder motivated by jealousy and distrust. And it's not just an old story. Today's news is full of stories of domestic violence prompted by betrayal, suspicion, and jealousy. And, today's couples have some new wrinkles on this old theme.

One of the new developments in marital infidelity and betrayal is the Internet, which I believe can tempt the vulnerable to take risks and jeopardize the trust in their relationships. New technology such as the Internet, instant messaging, PDAs, cell phone cameras, and the like make cybersex and other addictive activities (gambling, illicit relationships) much more accessible, and therefore more tempting. Inventive sales techniques such as seductive spam, hypersexual commercials (think of the lingerie commercials on TV), XXX-rated TV networks and cyber sites, make sex seem ever-present and encourage susceptible people to believe it's OK. Even obsessive involvement in online game-playing can cause a neglected spouse to feel jealous.

Temptation

Another dynamic that can damage trust is temptation. Feeling tempted and fantasizing can cause you to act in such a way that your partner feels suspicious and threatened. The most basic and common sign of temptation is a romantic charge that you feel and cannot deny, and whenever you see this special someone, somehow your day or evening brightens. Perhaps you work with him or her, or it's a friend of the family, or—horrors—your spouse's relative. At this point, you could defuse the attraction by taking one simple action—discuss it with your spouse. If you felt the ease or freedom to discuss it, you might discover what is driving the attraction. It may be a quality that your spouse once had that now lies fallow, or one that you and your spouse could foster, if only you knew what it was. By openly discussing the attraction without fighting and alienating one another, you and your spouse build trust and acknowledge that these things do happen and when they do, you'll deal with it because you are together for the long haul. If it's some-one at work, it may be that you and your spouse would decide it would be better for you to no longer go out to lunch alone with this person, or if it's a friend of the family, perhaps you agree that he or she should only visit the house when you're both home.

If the attraction is a friend or co-worker, meeting family members of the object of your fantasy does help to quell feel-ings of lust and longing.

"Once James and I were able to talk about my feelings, we decided to have lunch with Rick and his wife. After I met his wife and liked her, I realized that even if James and I were on our way to divorce court, I could not imagine acting on the attraction. The funny thing is, now I like his wife more than I like him. I could never be married to that guy with all his quirks. By getting to know her, and getting to know him better, the attraction fizzled, though we're still friends."

Temptation presents us with a dilemma because telling the truth is risky. Your partner may get angry or upset. But as long as the problem is only temptation, and you haven't done any-thing to act on it, telling the truth is much safer than withhold-ing. (If you have acted on your temptation, see the following section on infidelity and broken trust.) There are many excuses people use to avoid confessing:

- "I can't tell my partner the truth. It's too scary."
- "Instead of discussing what I'm feeling, I clam up, and then he (or she) thinks I'm hiding something."
- "My partner's self-esteem is too wobbly, and I don't want to hurt him (or her)."
- "My spouse is not open to talking and working things out. He (or she) won't listen."
- "How can I confess this attraction to my spouse without destroying our marriage?"

- "What if he or she becomes angry and rejects me?"
- "What if my partner never trusts me again?"

So instead of being honest, you become tongue-tied with worry that something has gone terribly off-kilter in your relationship. You may believe keeping your secret is a way to avoid being hurt, or hurting your partner. After all, you think, silence can never threaten what you have.

Still, it's difficult keeping such an exciting secret to yourself. The need to talk about it to someone is strong. Perhaps you pick a friend to talk to—preferably one who understands but not one who encourages you to go for it and asserts that life is much too short to bypass a little so-called harmless excitement. Unfortunately, with your emotion driving you, the tendency is to stay away from those who will provide sensible advice. In this state of mind, you probably don't want a friend to remind you to honor your commitment to your spouse, to forget about your new excitement and instead look more deeply at what may be at work and why this is happening. That would prick holes in the gorgeous fantasy you've created, one that you very much want—and think you need.

Worst of all, you may discuss it—perhaps at length—with the very person you should never discuss it with: the object of your fantasy. Sharing secrets creates a bond, and when you do this, the closeness increases between you and your new friend while the distance increases between you and your spouse.

"At first I didn't discuss James with Rick, or at least I voiced no complaints about my husband," says Kim. "Then I let it slip that he was gone a lot at night since he often teaches at night. Rick made a joke about it, and it seemed I enjoyed the attention Rick gave me and he seemed truly interested, so I started feeling freer voicing minor complaints. Rick lived in another county, and he was a customer, so there was never a question of him sneaking over or of us meeting secretly. Still, the attention via e-mail was welcome, and soon we were e-mailing daily. It didn't seem to be a huge problem—until I started e-mailing complaints about my marriage. How James didn't talk as much as I wish he did, or didn't get my jokes. Soon my dissatisfactions became Rick's and my little secret, drawing us closer. It was as if he was someone who understood and was there for me. Of course it was an illusion—he was not there for me at all, not really. But I imagined he was, and after all, that's what mattered at the time."

In this way, Kim began creating a rift between her and James, and, although she never had a sexual affair with Rick, the emotional connection between them, plus the secrecy, did damage to her marriage. Fortunately, Kim finally came in for therapy, and we developed a way for her to tell Rick of her temptation, which became the opening for solving her marital problems.

No matter what the cause of the disintegration of the trust between you, only one remedy will work—to confess and re-establish trust. As long as no infidelity has happened, and the problem is just temptation, suspicion, and/or damaged trust, you can use the following exercises to repair the problems and end the bickering.

SOLUTION
Repairing Damaged Trust

To repair damaged trust, both of you must be willing to take responsibility for your actions. Because people make mistakes, you can realistically expect that trust will be damaged occasionally during an extended relationship, due to misunderstanding or ignorance. Repairing broken trust requires emotional maturity and good negotiating skills; you must be able to discuss the angry and hurt feelings and work together to resolve them, with a therapist if necessary, so you can continue building healthy trust.

Trust is the basic underlying issue in all sexual matters of relationships. Do you trust yourself, and do you trust each other? On a surface level, a trusting relationship is one in which both partners feel secure that agreements will be honored. Behind this, however, is a much deeper issue: trusting each other to have self-control, and trusting your own selves. Trust, like all feelings, is difficult to pin down, to define. Trust of oneself is the basis of all trust. Although when our trust falters, most of us have the tendency to blame someone else (he cheated, she broke her word, you promised), the real issue at the root of trust is: Can I take care of myself if you let me down?

In order to have a trusting, reliable relationship with another person, you must be reliable and trustworthy yourself. If you make a promise to yourself, do you keep it? If you're unable to keep an agreement with yourself, no one else can trust you. In addition, your own untrustworthy behavior will lead you to believe that others are also unreliable. Your trust of your partner thus begins with your own self-esteem and self-control. The trust between you needs to develop in a reciprocal fashion, with each partner demonstrating to the other that trust expected is trust given. Reliability is crucial to the success of your relationship. If you're not sure how much you can trust your partner, back up, slow down, and begin to build that trust before going further. If you can't yet trust yourself—also back up, slow down, keep the relationship going slow until you repair the problem with yourself. If the trust between you and your partner has been damaged, you will need to work together to rebuild that trust. How do you build trust? Make agreements that are sensible, and keep them. Trust grows in a relationship over time, as contracts are kept. Be on time, pay your debts, and treat your partner with respect. When you can't keep your promise, say so in advance—if you can't do that, apologize and ask how you can repair the damage. The process is much the same whether you're building trust with yourself or someone else. The following guidelines will help you put these methods into practice:

Guidelines for Building Trust

1. Remember, fear breaks down trust. Don't frighten your partner (or yourself) by testing too hard, risking too much, or demanding the impossible. If you begin to feel frightened, talk about it. If you want to be told what is going on, don't make it too hard for your partner to be honest by making threats or reacting hysterically or with rage.

2. Keep each other informed. Lying or sneaking does even more damage than breaking contracts. If you slip up, tell the truth. If your partner errs, be open to hearing it without flying off the handle, and negotiate a solution to the problem, using the problem-solving steps in the first section of this chapter. If your partner keeps messing up and shows no sign of change, or if you can't keep your bargains, couples counseling is crucial. Do not delay, use the guidelines in chapter 9 and go immediately.

3. Learn to make clear contracts. And renegotiate them before you break them, as discussed in chapter 4.

4. Give it time. Patience and communication are your best allies. As you learn that you both make mistakes, and no one's being deliberately hurtful, trust builds. As it does, you can begin to relax the rules, and allow yourselves more spontaneity.

Had Kim not suppressed her initial sexual attraction, heartache may have resulted for her and James, and Rick and his wife, and countless others. Not to mention a possibility of losing Rick as a friend. Because she controlled her impulses, and because she and James were able to talk and work out a solution, their marriage is stronger and more loving.

Infidelity

In movies like *The Bridges of Madison County* and *Titanic* infidelity looks wonderfully romantic. In these depictions, to which the public obviously resonates, the dour, disapproving, or clueless spouse is the loser, and the illicit lovers win. Despite these romantic images, in real life infidelity causes pain, conflict, and broken families.

Magazine polls in both *Redbook* and *Cosmopolitan* have consistently shown that partners feel justified in cheating because they feel unloved, unappreciated, or disconnected, or they don't feel a partner is interested in them anymore. To a partner who is having a difficult time with intimacy, someone outside the marriage who is sympathetic and doesn't make demands can be very appealing.

Partners cheat because they are not sexually satisfied, there are problems or frustrations in the marriage, to stave off boredom and fear of aging, or because they don't feel emotionally fulfilled or valued. Either party might cheat if the marriage is disconnected, if they want to get "even," or if intimacy has sunk into friendship—affection without sex. People who are unable to work through difficult issues in their marriage, or who cannot maintain intimacy, often look elsewhere for comfort and reassurance.

> Kim says, "I had a crush on Rick when James and I were first dating, and now James doesn't seem able to trust me. He goes through my phone, and questions my every move. He always asks me, 'Did Rick call you today?' He knows it makes me irate. There is no reason for him not to trust me. I haven't done anything wrong, and I do love him and I want to work it out. A few months ago he told me that a woman at work was telling him that she liked him. All this makes me wonder if he's cheated on me to get back at me. He said he hasn't. But our relationship basically has no trust. We both need to learn how to control our tempers. I want to repair the trust in our relationship."

James says, "She's right, I don't really trust her. I hate all the anxiety and bickering, but I don't know how to be sure she's really faithful. I want to be able to trust my wife. I haven't cheated, but I am tempted. Why should I be loyal to her, if she's not to me? Why let her make a fool out of me?"

SITUATION

Broken Trust

Kim and James made their problem worse by not talking about it and by letting the guilt, anxiety, and resentment grow over time. The wish to avoid what is uncomfortable and difficult in your marriage by focusing on something light and easy outside is understandable, but avoidance will not help you create a marriage that is satisfying and happy. Couples come into my counseling office with various infidelity problems. Whether the marriage can be healed depends on how much damage exists in the marriage and how willing the partners are to take responsibility, to tell the truth, and to forgive each other.

In order to mend broken trust, both spouses need to be willing to talk openly about what went wrong, to take responsibility for what they did or didn't do to make the marriage work. It's an emotional maturity issue.

The good news is that couples can recover fully from infidelity if both partners are willing. I have counseled many who had a stronger relationship after the episode. Both partners must be willing to take responsibility for their own part (Kim must admit she made a mistake, James must acknowledge his anger and be willing to forgive) and develop new patterns of being together. It also takes a skilled therapist to keep them out of blaming/defending mode. If there has been an actual affair, the communicating and healing should be done with an established, qualified therapist, because it's too difficult to talk about this without someone to help maintain rationality. (If this has happened in your marriage, see the "Guidelines for Finding and Using Therapy Wisely" in chapter 9 for steps on how to begin couples counseling.)

Kim's mistake was innocent, early in her marriage. Instead of talking it through or getting counseling, they both tried to avoid the problem until it became too big to ignore. Now, they long for the easy connection they had before. As you read earlier in this chapter, they did eventually work it out, but they still needed to repair the trust between them by using the guidelines below, and getting help from a marriage counselor. In my experience with couples, I find that if a relationship has a good, solid basis, an occasional indiscretion may cause pain and upset, but it does not ruin the marriage. We tend to forgive those we love, even when they cause us pain.

Once trust has been broken, honest communication can revitalize a marriage by exposing the problems in it, opening up the communication, and eliminating the need for dishonesty. The pain suffered by the spouse who feels betrayed can be devastating, but once that pain is shared, and the time-honored process of confession, repentance, and forgiveness is completed, a couple can be stronger in their marriage than they were.

Weathering such a storm can create a stronger familial bond. A couple who work out their feelings together will survive as a family.

How to Heal from Infidelity

Most of us hope to create a long-standing marital and family relationship, and while we all hope never to have to deal with cheating and infidelity, it has been widespread in human relationships, despite terrible consequences, since the dawn of history. As painful as it might be to be cheated on, you may stand to lose a lot more if you cannot work it out, and have to give up many years' investment in an otherwise good relationship.

Not only is it possible to heal your relationship, it is also possible to begin anew, on a brand-new basis, and to develop a relationship that is temptation-resistant. The following guidelines and exercises will teach you the skills you were missing before.

Guidelines for Healing from Infidelity

If you encounter this kind of problem, here are some steps that will help you recover:

1. Get professional counseling help. It will be next to impossible to remain objective, whether you're the cheater or the one betrayed. A counselor will help you express and heal your pain, while moving the communication toward redemption and healing.

2. Be willing to hear each other. No matter how much you feel violated or misunderstood, finding out what your partner thinks and feels is the only way to work this out and heal it. Try to get your focus off blaming and accusing and on to finding out what happened, how everyone feels, and what to do next.

3. See the problem as your partner would. Each of you must try to understand the whole thing from the other's point of view. Imagine how your partner must feel, and talk about it, to begin to create a bridge between you.

4. Begin to rebuild trust. Begin to re-create the broken trust in your relationship by making simple promises and keeping them. If you have cheated, you have some repenting to do, and the best way to demonstrate your changed state of mind is to act in ways your partner finds reassuring. Allow your partner to monitor your behavior for a while with phone calls, and open up your communication. If you have been cheated on, avoid self-righteousness, and seek ways to find out how you can repair what was missing in the relationship.

5. Focus on solving the problem. Don't consider this healed until you can put it away forever. If it comes up whenever you have a problem, it will destroy what is left of the marriage. Keep working on your mutual communication, trust, and forgiveness until you know you have it repaired.

6. Open up your communication. To prevent infidelity from happening in the future, open up your communication until you can freely talk about being tempted, feeling unappreciated, and being resentful. These are the three things that most often lead to problems. If your sex life is less than satisfactory, seek sex counseling to improve it. Nothing makes temptation more powerful than feeling deprived.

7. Forgive and start over. When you have been successful in re-establishing your connection and growing trust, have a ceremony in which you formally forgive each other and agree to start fresh. Often couples renew their vows as a part of this step. You can use the "Guidelines for Building Trust" discussed earlier in this chapter.

Forgiving Your Partner

No matter how much you care, and how hard you try, when you get close to each other, you will occasionally get hurt. Even people who are responsible and care about each other make mistakes, because no one can be 100 percent aware, and because it's not always easy to understand what's important to another person. This emotional clumsiness can hurt, even when it's unintentional, so you need to know how to clear up the hurts when they happen. The power to resolve and let go of old hurts, while learning to protect yourself from being hurt again, is one of the most useful skills when it comes to intimate relationships.

True Forgiveness

Forgiveness is not easy. When you have truly forgiven there is no lingering resentment because the problem is solved. You have learned how to heal the hurt and prevent its recurrence, so you can forgive and wipe the slate clean. Knowing how to express feelings and figuring out a way to prevent a similar hurt from happening again makes it possible to forgive each other.

The dictionary defines *forgive* as "to give up resentment of" but my definition is a bit different. Giving up resentment is nearly impossible when there are too many real injuries to forgive. It can also be unwise, because resentment is a reminder to be careful around this person or in this situation. Letting go of resentment without fixing the problem makes you vulnerable to being hurt or mistreated over and over again.

Of course, hanging on to resentment will not protect you or allow you to let go of the past and move on. As long as you hold on to resentment, you will feel like a helpless, hopeless, dependent victim of your past history. You do need to learn to forgive, but just "giving up resentment" is not sufficient. You need a new model of forgiving.

EXERCISE: Steps to Forgiving

To forgive effectively, follow these main steps.

1. Understand why you're hurt. It's common to have hurt feelings and be disappointed but not know exactly what it's all about. What are you feeling? Are you angry at someone? What did he or she do? Are you sad? Why? Taking the time to get clear about your disappointment and hurt feelings will make it easier for you to be clear with your partner and easier for your partner to figure out what to do. If your partner did something wrong, just blaming still doesn't make it clear exactly how you were hurt, or what exactly you need to for-give your partner for.

2. Know how to take care of yourself. It seems very logical that if someone else hurt you, then that person should fix it. But it doesn't always work that way. If someone who loves you has hurt you, he or she either doesn't understand how you feel, isn't thinking clearly, or isn't in control of his or her own actions. This can be true in minor hurts and major ones. If your husband forgets your birthday, or your wife makes an important social date on the day of the big game, there may be several causes. If the error was due to faulty communica-tion or poor memory, you can take care of yourself by placing a calendar in a prominent location in your home and marking each important date, perhaps with different colored pencils to indicate whose memo it is. Technophiles can put in on their Palm Pilots. If a date is on the calendar, there are no "forget-ting" excuses.

If it's a very serious problem, get help. When it's clearly more than can be fixed by talking with each other, and you believe your partner is out of control (she burns dinner when she drinks too much, he gambles away a lot of money every payday, one of you has a drug addiction), you will need more than this book can provide, and I strongly recommend couples coun-seling and therapy or rehab targeted to the problem. See the "Guidelines for Finding and Using Therapy Wisely" in chapter 9. Go with or without your partner, and you will learn how to take care of yourself until he or she has better self-control. Until you know how to prevent yourself from being hurt again, forgiveness does not make sense.

3. Let your partner know how you feel. Once you are clear about how you were hurt or disappointed, you can be clear with your partner. Don't accuse—just speak in terms of your feelings. "My feelings were hurt when I didn't know where you were at the party." Or, "I'm disappointed because I wanted you to remember my birthday." Or, "When I found out you cheated, I felt unloved and worthless in your eyes."

4. Tell your partner what you think would fix the problem. When you offer a possible solution, your partner will have a clear idea of what you want. You can say, "When we go to parties, I'd like you to let me know where you are, and I want you to understand why I feel bad if you don't." Or, "I want you to keep me informed of where you are and what you're doing, and to allow me to call you at random times, until I'm reassured that you're keeping your promises."

5. Listen to your partner's version of what happened. Sometimes neither you nor your partner has really broken trust, and the problems are caused mainly by a difference in perception, so it's important to understand how your partner saw the situation. This also keeps the discussion on a more even level, with both partners discussing the problem rather than one accusing and the other defending. You may learn that your partner even thought he or she was doing something you wanted. "You kept saying you didn't want to celebrate this birthday, and I thought you meant it." Or, "You never wanted to have sex with me, so I thought you'd be OK with me going somewhere else." Whether you like what you hear or not, the only chance you have to solve the problem is to listen and seek to understand.

6. Reach a mutual solution to the problem. If someone is very hurt, or very defensive, it may take a few discussions to resolve this problem. Remember that it is worth the time it takes because it will prevent this from becoming a recurring problem. If you can't solve it together after a few tries, see a counselor. Forgiveness skills are so important that you really need to learn them if you haven't already.

7. Have a forgiving ceremony. This can be as simple as looking into your partner's eyes and saying "I forgive you" or as complicated as renewing your vows after the problem is solved. What's important is that you communicate that the air is cleared, the hurt forgiven, and the problem is over. You won't be able to do that honestly if you haven't done the previous steps.

You don't have to condemn your partner to be wary of his or her out-of-control or thoughtless behavior. Instead, you can recognize that both of you are fallible human beings, do what is necessary to fix the problems, and then forgive each other. When both of you take responsibility for fixing these mistakes in the relationship, your trust in each other will grow, and where trust grows, so does love.

Building a Temptation-Resistant Marriage

The best thing to do about temptation and infidelity is to prevent it in the first place. The most important way to resist temptation is to make sure the sex and romance stay alive and vital within your relationship. As stated earlier in this chapter, in the section on developing transitions, it's easy to feel romantic when you live separately and date each other because every moment spent together is special. From the moment you begin to live together, such romantic moments are no longer automatic. Instead, much of your time together is spent on more mundane things: doing laundry, washing dishes, paying bills, or going to work. Although this can be new, exciting, and fun at first, as soon as the initial newness of living together wears off, such everyday things cease to feel exciting and romantic, and you may find yourself feeling worried that your partner no longer cares as much or is as excited to be with you. One way to combat this problem is to follow the "Guidelines for Increasing Intimacy" given earlier in this chapter, and then use the following exercise.

To protect your marriage against infidelity, temptation, and secrecy, you can learn to be more realistic about your sexual connection. When your relationship lasts for a while, your lovemaking will change. As you get closer, passion no longer grows automatically out of the excitement of the new and unknown. Your sexual connection becomes deeper and more secure, but less exciting, because passion and excitement are related to insecurity and to the newness of the relationship. Once you've established a reliable, comforting connection based on trust, insecurity and excitement fade, and it's easy to take your love for granted. The following guidelines will help you add some fun, excitement, and newness to your sexual relationship.

Guidelines for Creating a Sexual Repertoire

Rather than allowing your energy to subside, you can allow your lovemaking to change and grow, deepening as your partnership does. Couples who develop a "sexual repertoire" that includes a variety of sexual habits, attitudes, and options report feeling more satisfaction and freedom to express their love, with enough variety that they never get bored.

These suggestions will help you create a variety of experiences together:

- "Quickies" are ways you have sex when you don't really have time for a full, leisurely romantic evening: one of you giving oral sex before you leave for work, petting to climax in the car at a drive-in movie, using vibrators to have orgasms without a lot of foreplay late at night, taking a nap and having a "quickie" before rushing off to a party.
- Sneaky sex has the added excitement of "forbidden fruit": having silent sex behind locked doors while the children are watching TV, sneaking lovemaking in your childhood bedroom while visiting your parents, visiting your partner at work and having quickie sex on the couch in a locked office.
- Romantic sex is the full-blown variety: candlelight, dinner, quiet talking, dressing up, perhaps a lovely hotel room, or a romantic dinner for two when you have time alone at

home. Especially good for anniversaries, Valentine's Day, or anytime your relationship needs a boost.

- New couple sex is recreating a scene from your dating days as closely as possible: the time you met at church and couldn't wait to get home and make love, the flowers you used to bring home as a surprise, or saying all the silly, wildly-in-love things you said then.
- Make-up sex after you've had an argument or a struggle and forgiven each other can be extra tender and memorable.
- Comfort sex is for when one of you is sad or stressed. The other partner is especially caring and soothing, doing everything to comfort and relax the suffering one.
- Relaxing sex is the kind to do on a weekend morning, when you have no obligations, and can laze around, have breakfast in bed, and make love for as long as you want: no pressure, no hurry, and no demands on each other.
- Reassuring sex is affection and intimacy intended to reassure a partner who is temporarily insecure. It reaffirms your mutual love and commitment to each other and is often accompanied by many verbal declarations of love and explaining again why you are so important to each other.
- Fantasy sex acts out all the silly, forbidden, or exciting fantasies: nurse and patient; two little children "playing house"; master or dominatrix and slave; stripper and customer; extraterrestrial alien and abductee; famous movie star and adoring fan; your two favorite characters from a soap opera, novel, or movie; or anything else you can imagine. This is a great time for costumes, masks, sexual toys, leather outfits, or whatever enhancements you enjoy.

The possible varieties of sexual attitudes, environments, energies, and activities are truly endless. No matter how exciting any of the above options seems at first, if it is all you do, it will become boring eventually, and no matter how tame the alternative is, if you haven't done it for a while, it will refresh and revitalize your experience of each other. By spicing up your love life with occasional surprises, you can enhance your connection with a little excitement and fun.

Chapter 4

SOLVING KIDS SQUABBLES

Of all the arguments married couples can have, the fights about children can be the most intense and complex, and if the underlying problems are not solved, the fights can last a lifetime, even after divorce.

Raising children is the most complicated, puzzling, and hopefully rewarding job a couple can have. It is also a huge responsibility, and, because it can be stressful and mysterious, one of the biggest sources of struggle in marriages. In many instances, the struggles begin from the moment the baby arrives. With the extended family and the neighborhood no longer being sources of assistance, and with the increase of single-child, single-parent families, new parents often lack support or a realistic idea of what parenting a child entails. Furthermore, they often lack models for how to parent, or the models they saw in their own families may not fit their lives today. This chapter will not tell you how to parent your children, but it will show you how to stop fighting about them.

STRUGGLE
To Have Children or Not

Struggling over children can begin before you're even pregnant if one of you wants children and the other doesn't, or if you have differing ideas about what parenting means.

> Harold and Cassandra both had burgeoning law careers and met when they were both working at the same firm. Their relationship went smoothly, until shortly after they were married and began talking about having children. Harold really wanted children, but Cassandra didn't want to give up her career. She said: "I might want children someday, but right now I love being a successful lawyer. I worked hard to get here. I don't want to take time off to have children right now. It would put me on a 'mommy track' and I'm afraid my career would never be the same." Harold says, "I wish we had talked about this more specifically before we got married. I see now that we were vague about children. I'm afraid that both Cassie and I will regret it if we wait too long."

SITUATION
Life-Changing Decision

If Harold and Cassandra turn this problem into a fight about who's right and who's wrong, they will never reach a satisfactory solution. Whether they have children or not, they will create resentment and hurt feelings that will last a long time. Whether or not to have children is a very big decision, and Cassandra is right that parenting responsibilities often fall most heavily on the mom and that taking time out for childbearing and rearing can significantly derail her career. But if, like Harold and Cassie, you both want children, you can work together to find solutions to the problem.

You and your partner may both want to have children, but your timing, priorities, and expectations may be different. One person's priorities may be focused on having financial security before having a family. Or perhaps you feel you still haven't had enough time to enjoy your relationship as a couple before adding extra responsibility, while your partner is eager to begin a family. This timing difference can lead to big fights about when (or whether) to have a child. Surprisingly enough, the difference between fighting and working it out usually is understanding the details of what your partner feels about the issue.

- **It might be a financial problem:** "To raise a child right is very expensive, from doctor bills to babysitting right through college. I'd like to make sure we have a solid financial foundation before we have a child."
- **A timing problem:** "Yes, I'd like to have children, but I don't feel ready to be a mom (or dad) yet. I want us to have some more fun (or I want to develop my career) first."
- **A fear problem:** "I always thought I'd like children, but now that the time has come, I'm afraid I won't be good at parenting (or patient enough, or I'm afraid I'll turn into my angry father)."
- **A disruption problem:** "I really like our life right now, I'm happy in my career, I don't want all that change."
- **A love (time, or sex) scarcity problem:** "I'm afraid that, when we have children, you'll give all your time and attention to them, and have none for me."
- **A family problem:** "As long as we have to live so far from my family, I don't think I have enough support to be a parent." Or, "My own childhood was so difficult, I'm doubtful that I can give my children the support they need. I'm afraid I'll be inadequate as a parent."

Each of these problems has solutions as long as you clearly understand what's in the way. The key to working out agreements about having children is to understand each other. Instead of reacting to each other, seek to understand your partner's point of view, and to express your own feelings and thoughts.

SOLUTION

Understanding Each Other

If you are having a fight about whether or not to have children, it's probably not as difficult as you think to arrive at a workable solution. To do this, you need to have a listening session. In the previous chapters, you have learned some skills and guidelines to help you take the time to talk about sensitive subjects in a caring fashion. The following guidelines will help you make sure you and your partner understand each other when the topic is difficult.

Guidelines for Being Better Understood

1. Seek first to understand. If you know your partner's frame of reference or the inner issues he or she has, you can speak to him or her in language that will make sure you are understood. The common reaction to a problem is to insist on explaining your own point of view over and over, to convince your partner your opinion is the right one. Instead of hearing each other, you wind up talking louder and louder in a futile attempt to be heard, until you're yelling at each other. No one is listening. If, instead, you focus on hearing and listening until you understand what your partner is saying, and then you repeat your partner's thoughts in your own words, both of you will relax and the problem will be a lot less scary. So stop and think whether you want to be right or you want to solve the problem. Trying to be right will not get you where you want to go.

2. Pay attention to how your words are landing. In the previous step, when you repeat back what your partner said, you're doing active listening, letting your partner know what you heard him or her say. The other side of this is what I call "attentive speaking." That is, paying attention to how your partner is reacting to what you're saying. As you're talking, watch your partner's face, eyes, and body language to see how what you're saying is being received. If your companion's response looks off the mark for what you said (for example, you're trying to be helpful and your sweetheart looks upset or hurt), check out what he or she is hearing. Maybe what you tried to communicate was misheard, misunderstood, or misconstrued. If you stop when you see evidence that you aren't getting through, and ask a question (Do you agree? What do you think?), you'll get a lot farther with your communication. Attentive speaking is such an important skill that I've explained it in more detail, with steps you can follow, in chapter 5 (page 135). Refer to that section if you need more explanation of this powerful tool.

3. Focus on the solution. Rather than describe or complain about the problem over and over, switch your focus to finding a solution that will work for both of you. Only focus on the problem long enough to understand; then move to what will fix it. If this has been a problem for a while, you've probably both described it to each other many times. It's always easier to repeat your litany of woe and sound like a whiner or a nag than it is to stop and think about possible solutions. But keep in mind that complaining will cause your partner to stop listening to you. Also, focusing too long on the problem will cause both of you to feel blamed and criticized. Instead, as soon as you understand both sides of the problem (which only takes a few minutes if you're really listening) say, "OK, I get that the problem is _____. What do you think will fix it?"

4. Separate emotion from solution. When you have a difficult problem, it's natural for one or both of you to be emotional. It's common to have hurt feelings, to be afraid the problem can't be solved, to get angry or frustrated. However, when either or both of you is upset, irrational, or reactive, you aren't communicating. You cannot think clearly when you are upset and flooded with "fight or flight" hormones. Remember, the minute you get upset, you've lost your ability to find a solution. Take a break and try again in a few minutes, when both of you have calmed down. If necessary, use the "time-out" technique that follows these guidelines.

5. Don't beat dead horses. If you've been over the same discussion several times, and you're stuck with no forward movement, try a different approach. If you cannot come up with a different approach on your own, consider getting some help. Don't just keep having dead-end arguments. If you do that, you'll develop a habit pattern that will be difficult to break. If you and your partner cannot find a solution or come to an agreement within a few days, consider going to your clergyperson or a professional counselor for help. A trained professional is not emotionally involved in the situation and can be objective, which means he or she can think clearly and help you develop more solutions. An objective third party can work wonders, and the quicker you go, the easier (and cheaper) it will be to reach a solution. Use the "Guidelines for Finding and Using Therapy Wisely" in chapter 9.

6. Be nice. Grandma's adage, "You get more flies with honey than with vinegar" is very useful when you want to be heard. If you keep in mind that the person you are talking to is not your enemy, but your life partner, you'll communicate more gently and with more care. Guard against competing or being right. The point of your discussion is to create understanding that goes both ways.

Cassandra says: "When I think about being successful at getting what I want, I remember that in the school lunchroom, when I had a bologna sandwich, and my friend had PB&J, I had a better chance of getting the half sandwich I wanted from her if I offered to share my half sandwich first. So, if I want my husband to listen to me, I use the same tactic. I offer to consider what he wants if he'll consider what I want. The nicer I am, the better chance I have of getting through to him."

When you interact with these guidelines in mind, you'll find out what's really behind your partner's feelings and reactions, and when you know that, it's easier than you think to solve the problem.

Once Harold and Cassie stopped arguing and began listening to each other, and Harold understood Cassie's concern that she'd lose her law career, he suggested that they begin trying to have a child, which would mean Cassie could work until she was pregnant and close to term. He also promised Cassie that, when she was ready, they'd start a private legal practice of their own. She could work as much or as little as she wanted, and he would also help with childcare as much as he could. This idea appealed to Cassie because she could do a lot of work from home and care for the children without giving up her legal career.

Bonus Guidelines: How to Take a Time-Out

Whenever an argument becomes too heated, and you are aware that you're saying the same things you've said before, things have deteriorated into blaming and defending, or someone is getting very upset, it's useful to take a time-out. This works very much as it does in basketball, where everyone can be running full tilt down the court and someone makes the "T" sign with one hand perpendicular to the other, and the action stops immediately. You can even use the same signal.

To Call Time-Out:

1. Make an agreed-upon sign. Some couples make the "T" symbol with their hands; some choose a "safe" word, a nonsense word that wouldn't be used often, like "rutabaga." Others use a word that has significance to both parties, such as "Palm Springs" to recall a time they stopped fighting on vacation. Or "overload" to indicate that they think things have gotten too intense. When you're not fighting, choose what sign you'll use during a fight, and honor your agreement that when one of you says the word or makes the sign, both of you have to stop talking.

2. Walk away. Giving the signal means both of you agree to stop fighting immediately and walk away. You can just go to separate rooms, one of you can take a walk or a shower, or you both can just go write out your anger. The point is to get out of each other's sight for an agreed-upon time. Built into your agreement about time-outs is a specific break time. Twenty minutes is usually enough time for both parties to calm down, get past the reactionary anger, and begin to think more rationally.

3. Come back together. After your break, come back together and resume the discussion. It usually works well to make the agreement that the person who called time-out will open the discussion again. It's important to come back to the problem, so the time-out process doesn't become a way to win an argument. You may find it necessary to call time-out more than once in a heated argument. Don't hesitate to do it as often as necessary. It's better to break up the discussion than to deteriorate into fighting. If you take frequent breaks, you'll change your pattern from arguing to calmly discussing the problem.

STRUGGLE

Having a Baby Ruined Our Relationship

A new baby changes everything about your life—sleep schedules, priorities, your social life, your financial status, and the primary couple relationship. These changes happen overnight, because the day a baby is born, everything is different from the day before. There is no way to accurately predict how these changes will feel, and the learning curve for new parents is very steep. Stepparenting and blended families, the adolescent years, and struggles about parenting styles add to the potential for struggle. Here are some of the major disagreements couples have about their children, and how to fix them.

New parents may not realize how vital it is to be around an experienced parent.

> When stay-at-home mom Lucy had her first baby, her mom, who had raised three children of her own, came to visit and help with the new baby. She arrived at the house to find Lucy at her wits' end with a screaming baby in her arms. Grandma put down her suitcase, held out her arms, and said, "Let me hold him." Lucy handed her infant son over, and Grandma had him quieted down in three minutes. Lucy's husband Greg was astounded. "How did you do that?" He asked. Grandma smiled and said "experience." During the next two weeks, she gave Lucy the benefit of her experience and was available by phone whenever she was needed. Today, Lucy says, "I have no idea what I would have done without her. The books just don't teach you how it feels, how to intuit what the baby wants, and so many other things my mother knows from experience. I didn't really appreciate my mom's expertise until I became a mother myself."

Couples who don't have the support of knowledgeable family members who are experienced parents can be overwhelmed and panicky when they have their first direct experience of how demanding being a new parent can be. Babies absorb enormous amounts of time, attention, and emotional energy.

> About three weeks after Lucy's child was born, she said, "I woke up this morning and realized: Oh. It's EVERY day." She had just realized on an emotional level (although she knew intellectually) that there are no days off from parental responsibility, and what that actually meant in terms of change in her life. Greg, in the meantime, was having his own reactions. "Where has my wonderful wife gone? We haven't had sex for months, first because it was the last few weeks of the pregnancy, then the doctor said no sex right after the birth, and now Lucy is so exhausted from childcare and nighttime feedings. I hate to say it, but the baby is like a little vampire that sucks not only Lucy's milk, but also her time, energy, and love. How long does this last? When will I get my wife back?"

SITUATION
Overwhelmed

Even couples who look forward eagerly to their first child will experience "baby shock"—the disorientation and dismay of dealing with the reality, rather than the fantasy, of having a baby. Couples who are not thrilled to be pregnant may be even more upset. If you are contemplating having a child, to minimize the shock of caring for a newborn, get as much real baby experience as possible beforehand. Offer to babysit for friends or family members for a few days at a time, or longer if possible, so you get to see how much work and know-how is involved. Take parenting classes together before the baby is born, so you'll have a mutually understood format for discussing child rearing issues. Make sure you discuss the difficult things about raising a baby before the baby arrives. Talk to other new parents. None of this will be the same as having your own child, which carries with it a much greater responsibility, but it will give you a more realistic idea of what's to come. Understand that the couple relationship you're accustomed to will be put on hold for the first few months, until the baby is sleeping through the night, although if you share care of your baby together, you'll bond with each other as well as your child.

SOLUTION
Get Information and Support

Whenever you can, learn from more experienced parents, whether they are part of the family or not. A connection with other parents will greatly reduce your anxiety and also give you a chance to take a break from time to time. Your relationship will not be a priority during this time, so the more realistic you are about this beforehand, the less resentful you'll be when it happens. Once things have settled down, the mother has recovered from giving birth, the baby is sleeping through the night, and you've established a routine, things will become more manageable.

As much as possible, organize your schedule so that you have some time together, without having to do chores or work, after the baby is asleep. Talk frequently together about how you're both doing, whether your arrangement feels fair, and encourage each other to talk about anything that may be bothering you. Each of the previous chapters has had suggestions to help you express difficult issues to each other, and if you use them in this situation, you have an opportunity to fix problems before they become worse.

Take a Break
One of the biggest pitfalls for new parents is to focus on being parents too much and lose their couple connection. It is so easy for your original partnership to take a backseat to the

demands of parenting that this is an excellent time to establish a tradition that focuses on maintaining your couple relationship. As soon as you can arrange for someone trustworthy to babysit (it is often difficult for a new mother to relinquish control, but you'll find a break from the baby is worth the stretch), take at least one night out a week together, or, if the baby can go to grandma's or a trusted relative or friend's house, you can have an intimate, quiet night at home. Use this time to relax, reconnect, and talk over what's been going on during the week. If you do this on a regular basis, it will become familiar, and not overblown. The point is not to have a "once in a lifetime" event, but to set up a regular, relaxed time for being together. You can choose to go out somewhere fancy if you like, but being at home in comfy clothes is fine, too, as long as it's an opportunity to be together and talk.

Each of you needs time for yourself, too. Hopefully both of you will take part in childcare, which keeps the burden from being too great on one parent. If you both contribute equally, each of you can then have one night off while the other watches the child. This time by yourself will refresh you both for childcare and for your relationship.

Create a Parents' Group

The most effective thing new parents can do is to make friends with other parents. A social group of peers will give you so many new options. You can trade childcare with other parents (one couple watches both children, and the other gets a night out) or spend social time with other parents (several couples meet at the house of one couple, and the children come along and go to sleep there at bedtime so the adults can spend some time together) and it's an inexpensive and supportive way to socialize.

A parenting network will give you:

- An interested and sympathetic forum to share medical, parenting, and development concerns
- An audience that is actually interested in the amazing accomplishments of your children
- Knowledgeable and experienced sources of advice and referral to pediatricians, childcare, shopping resources, books, health, food, and other parenting info
- A peer group that shares your experiences and understands your needs
- A social group that understands the limits parenting puts on your socialization
- Other moms and dads who want to take all your and their children to the same places together
- An all-important peer group for your children as they develop and go to school, an "extended family," that the children can say they "grew up with" even if your genetic family lives far away

When you nurture your couple relationship and find support as parents, you'll take a lot of the stress and pressure out of parenting. Until you experience it, you won't know what a relief it can be to call up a good friend when you're worried about your child, your parenting decisions, or a problem in your marriage, and hear that friend say, "Oh, yes, that happened to me, and here's what I did about it. It'll be OK."

STRUGGLE
Discipline, Punishment, and Parenting Styles

The biggest source of kid struggles arises in the everyday problems of parenting, child management, and discipline. The most successful couples understand that parenting is a highly demanding (as well as rewarding) occupation, and discuss their preferences, values, differences, and experiences beforehand. Unfortunately, before having children, too many couples just fantasize about the joys of parenthood and forget to talk about the difficult aspects, such as whether they agree on discipline, values, and financial issues (e.g., private school vs. public school) before the children arrive. We've all seen shows like *The Super Nanny* where parents are clueless about parenting their children and the nanny comes in and shows them techniques that magically work. It's not as mysterious as it seems. The best nannies have a lot of training and education in child development and behavior. Unfortunately, parents seem to have the expectation that they'll know what to do, or that they'll do better than their own parents did.

Given the confusion and lack of information many parents have, it's surprising that so many parents manage to do OK. But, if things don't go well, parents who are confused or under stress can really do damage to themselves, their relationships, and their children. Even when parents are doing relatively well with their children, arguments can develop.

Parenting children, added to earning a living and maintaining your marriage and your home, can be an overwhelming responsibility. As parents, just trying to make it through your days, you can fall into patterns that seem to work, but don't feel quite right.

"My three kids adore my husband, Mike," says Daisy, "and it's no wonder since he spends a lot of time hanging out and goofing around with them. But the flip side is that he leaves the disciplinary duties up to me, so the kids see me as the serious, bossy one. How can I get Mike to share the load so the kids get to see my fun-loving side?"

Mike clearly loves his children, so Daisy is confused. How can she complain about such a great dad? But on the other hand, the way things have worked out, she feels that the situation is very unfair.

Mike says: "I longed for a fun-time dad when I was a kid, so now I'm trying to give that to the children. My dad was tough, way too hard on me, and I'm afraid to discipline my kids. I'm worried that I might go overboard. I love playing with them, but I won't try to make them follow Daisy's rules. I know it's not fair to her, but I'm no good at that part."

SITUATION
Are Our Responsibilities Fair?

Mike is clearly worried that he can't discipline appropriately, so he has left all the discipline to his wife. Problems with division of labor and fairness often come from ideas and prejudices learned in the early family. Both partners can believe that the mother should raise the children and the dad earn the paycheck, and if they both enjoy their responsibilities, that can work fine. But when mom works and still winds up doing most of the chores and parenting, then things begin to feel unfair. Also, gender and role differences can play a part. Dr. Wade F. Horn, president of the National Fatherhood Initiative, writes:

Mothers and fathers . . . parent differently. . . . Mothers, for example, tend to be more verbal with their children, whereas fathers are more physical. Mothers tend to talk more to their infants and to sing songs to them. Fathers like to roll around with their infants on the floor. . . . Mothers tend to encourage more caution, whereas fathers urge more achievement and independence. . . . Fathers tend to be more results-oriented and less sensitive to the pleadings of children, whereas moms are more focused on the emotional experience of their children. . . . Fathers tend to be more focused than moms on helping their children learn about the world outside the family. Once their babies are old enough, for example, dads like to carry their infants facing outward, whereas moms are more likely to continue to hold their infants facing inward. Later, dads tend to emphasize the importance of learning life's hard lessons, believing those lessons will help their children be successful when they become adults. Moms tend to be more concerned about protecting their children and keeping them close to the family. These differences can lead to the "wait till your father gets home" scenario of mom being the permissive parent and dad being the disciplinarian. If someone in your house feels that all the responsibility and work is on his or her shoulders, the problem can be worked out and fixed.

SOLUTION
Write It Down

When you're arguing about the division of parenting and discipline in your family, as with every other problem, sitting down and talking about it is the key to solving the problem. Instead of stewing or bickering about things being unfair, try getting clear about what each of you is actually doing. It's possible your duties aren't as out of balance as you think, and you're just not understanding all your partner does. Or, perhaps your partner is holding off and letting you do what you're doing because he or she believes you want it that way.

Writing Down Responsibilities

The only way to find out is to write down all the duties you see each of you doing. Perhaps, for example, you feel responsible for making sure homework is done; for imposing penalties (like grounding or taking away privileges) when a child breaks the rules; or for getting everyone up, dressed, fed, and out of the house in time for school. If that's the case, write down all you do, and then write down what you think your partner does. Then, ask your partner to do the same thing. Sometimes, looking at each other's lists without arguing is all that's needed to see how to balance out the situation. If you need to work out some more mutually satisfying solutions, use the problem solving method on page 41. Focus on how you can be helpful to each other, and balance the power and responsibilities between you.

> Daisy sat down to figure out specifically what felt unfair to her. When she did, she decided she needed Mike to help her enforce the rules and keep order in the house. "I said to Mike, 'I need your help with the kids. You do a great job of playing with them, and they love you, but I could use some help enforcing the rules. Do you agree with me about what the rules should be?'"
>
> Mike was receptive when Daisy approached him to solve the problem, rather than complain. He said, "You're so good at parenting and discipline, and I don't feel like I know what to do. Please help me by asking me to help in simple, specific ways. Please don't assume that I know what to do. I don't." Daisy began saying things like "Kara needs help studying for her vocabulary quiz. I know she'd get a great grade on it if you drilled her." The next time their boys were struggling, Daisy said, "Mike, show them how a man settles an argument." As he took on parenting as well as playing, he gained more confidence in his ability, and Daisy made sure to compliment him on being a great father.
>
> Mike loved it when he realized that his kids needed his guidance. Mike also suggested to Daisy, that when her instincts began leading her to taking on her "bad cop" role, she could choose to simply smile and tell the kids, "We can play for an hour, but then it's homework time." In this way, Daisy got to be the playtime parent too, without letting the kids' duties slide.

STRUGGLE
Parenting Rules and Styles

New parents are often shocked to discover they disagree about how to raise their child. Established parents who have been agreeing all along can suddenly find themselves at a disagreement about proper parenting when their child hits a certain age or situation, such as going to school, or entering adolescence; or they are surprised to find they disagree about how to raise boys, when they did fine with girls, or vice versa. Also, your joint parenting style may go fine as long as the children are doing OK but become a problem when you feel inadequate because your child is having problems (social or academic) at school or contracts a difficult illness. Under pressure, it's easy to begin to fight about who knows best how to parent, but sliding into another right/wrong argument will only make the problem worse.

SITUATION
Many Different Strategies

No matter why you are disagreeing about how to parent your children, it is important to keep in mind that there are many different successful strategies for parenting children, not just one right one. Different situations and different children may require different parenting rules and styles. Understanding what your children are doing developmentally can make a huge difference in parenting success. I recommend to parents in my counseling practice that they take parenting classes—partly to learn the information, partly so you'll have a new system of discipline and management that you both understand, and partly because it eliminates a lot of parental struggles about whose family did it "the right way."

SOLUTION
Find a Common Ground

One way of ending the struggle is to agree that what you need to do is to raise your children to be successful adults and to focus on your child's success in the world; that is, in business, relationships, and in discovering meaning in life. If your child doesn't learn self-control and how to handle disappointment now, he or she will struggle throughout adult life. As parents, you are not there to please your child or make your child happy, but to teach and prepare that child for a successful adult life. A child is not your friend or your burden, but your responsibility (and hopefully, your joy) to rear appropriately. Do not allow your children to beg and plead, it's not good for them or for you. Parents need a plan, and to figure out how to agree about when to say "yes" and when to say "no." When both parents are in agreement, children can't use one against the other. The earlier you get in charge and sort out these problems, the easier your parenting tasks will be. The end result is children who respect and love you and who have the skills they need to maintain relationships and to achieve their goals in life.

Another option is to consult your extended family, and the experienced parents you both agree are the best, and ask their advice. Support from more experienced parents can really help you solve the struggles you're having about how to handle your children.

If you cannot reach an agreement, research some parenting classes (try *www.parentingonline.org* or *http://childparenting .about.com/od/parentingeducation/* for online help, or look for family services in your phonebook or ask your school counselor). Ask your spouse to take a class with you, either online or in person, so the two of you can have the same goals and language for parenting your children. Taking a class prevents a "who's right" fight between you, and gives you a shared language for thinking and talking about what you need to do as parents.

Couples who take parenting classes together before having children report that they acquire a common language and foundation that makes future decisions much easier.

STRUGGLE

Clash of Faith

Very often, couples take their religious beliefs and background lightly until they have children. As adults, many couples can give each other the space to have different beliefs, even to go to different services or practice different rituals and holidays. But, when children come into the picture, things change abruptly. Suddenly, parents feel that they are fighting for the souls of their children. Some religions mandate how children must be raised in a mixed family. Families can get involved in the struggle, too.

Jan and Ron have known each other since they were teenagers and high school sweethearts, so they thought they knew each other well. They did well in the first months of their marriage, and they were eager to be parents, so they were thrilled when Jan got pregnant right away, and a second time when their firstborn son was about a year old. Although raising two young children kept them busy, they were happy to be a growing family. Suddenly, when their son reached school age, a problem arose that they hadn't anticipated. Jan was Catholic, and Ron Jewish, which had not been a problem when they were dating. Neither attended services regularly. They were able to join each other's family celebrations, ceremonies, and weddings without a problem. Their own wedding combined religious rituals and ceremonies, with a liberal rabbi and priest sharing the officiating. Their families were a little skeptical, but because they knew how much Jan and Ron cared about each other, and because neither family was strictly observant, they went along.

Both Jan and Ron were surprised when each of them wanted their children raised as they were, with a religious education. Furthermore, they each were shocked at the intensity of their feelings. Because both families' religions put a lot of emphasis on raising children in their religion, with rituals like Catholic Catechism, First Communion, and Confirmation, and Jewish Hebrew school and Bar or Bat Mitzvahs, the issue became a fierce debate.

Their problem is not unusual. Wade Clark Roof, chair of the department of religious studies at the University of California at Santa Barbara says, "New patterns are emerging . . . churches and synagogues are already accommodating these realities, and will continue to do so."

According to the *Journal of Marriage & the Family*, 50 percent of Jews marry non-Jews, and half of Catholics marry non-Catholics. And the church has been accommodating it for quite a while. In 1997, according to the *Official Catholic Directory*, 30 percent of the marriages blessed by the Catholic Church involved interfaith couples.

SITUATION
Religion More Important for Parents

When you're in love, happy, and excited, issues like differences in religion don't seem to be a big problem. For some couples, the issue does arise when they get married, especially if they have a big wedding involving family and friends. Even so, it's not too difficult to find a compromise such as a secular, mixed religious, or nondenominational ceremony. But adults who can be rational about their own personal faith, or can ignore faith for themselves, often find they cannot feel the same detachment when it comes to questions of how (or even whether) to bring their children up in a faith. This problem is intensified when there is a component of criticism of each other's religion. If one or both of you believes that your faith is the "one, true belief," or if you believe that your partner's beliefs are not valid or serious, that dismissive attitude can lead to explosive arguments. Religion is a loaded subject because it has such profound emotional, historical, ancestral, and social meaning. Religion may lie dormant when everything is going smoothly, but as the saying goes "there are no atheists in foxholes." When we are under stress or pressure, most people turn to religion for support and meaning. We can keep our faith to ourselves when it's only about us, in fact most people believe faith should be a private matter. But, having children brings it all up to the surface. Because most people do have a foundation of faith in the back of their minds to draw on in times of need, they want their children to have the same support. Also, parents usually think that religious education is necessary to give children a moral foundation, with guidelines to follow about right and wrong. On the other hand, some people who are atheist or agnostic and regard religion as a negative influence are determined that their children be raised religion free. Fights about these issues can be devastating and intractable, and religion can be a very touchy issue for couples. Not only is it a personal choice, it also has generations of tradition and family pressure behind it. Religion is an emotionally laden topic, heavy with family and cultural history. In fact, research shows that culture is the biggest determining factor in what religion people follow. So, differences in religion can be very difficult to sort out. Couples who have these differences need to consider all possibilities, including blending religious traditions, in order to reach a workable place.

Most clergy are not as adamant about these issues as individuals can be; every sizable community has an ecumenical council, at which members of all faiths meet to promote tolerance and interfaith communication. Usually, a responsible spiritual counselor will focus on preserving the family, even if it means compromising some rules. Unfortunately, many of these fights come down to "my belief is better than your belief," which is a fight no one can win.

SOLUTION
Creative Blending

Seeking understanding and unity, which are basic tenets of most religions, are the attitudes that will lead to solving problems of religion and how to give your children a religious background. "Interfaith families who take the religious development of their children seriously can model healthy and respectful pluralism. They can live out what should be the goal for society as a whole," maintains Darrel H. Jodock of Gustavus Adolphus College in St. Peter, Minnesota, who focuses on religious trends in America and Jewish-Christian relations. When you learn about each other's faith (or nonreligious beliefs) in a spirit of acceptance and tolerance you can then create a blend of your own. Of course, it's easiest if this is done before having children, because the stakes don't seem as high, but couples don't often think of this ahead of time. Your relationship and your family bonding will benefit when you learn to overcome your differences: "Trimming the Christmas tree or lighting menorah candles together may strengthen your marriage," said Syracuse University psychology professor Barbara Fiese, who interviewed 120 couples about the particulars of their religious holiday rituals. "We have found that couples who embrace their rituals reaffirm beliefs as well as a relationship."

Guidelines for Resolving or Blending Religious Differences

When you and your partner disagree about faith, you may have great difficulty resolving the issue because it has so much meaning for each of you, and also because your family pressures and obligations affect the decision. If one of you is disinterested and the other deems faith important, you may wind up having a power struggle about the children and the extended family. Resolving this requires understanding exactly what is important to each partner. Is it what the family will think? Is it concern that the difference will separate you? The following guidelines will help you resolve your religious differences and the question of how to raise your children.

1. Agree to resolve the issue: Do what it takes to figure out how to work together on this, rather than fight about it. Understand that raising your children with good values can happen no matter which religion or belief you frame those values in, and that having a good, working partnership is more important to your own happiness and your children's well-being than any particular set of beliefs, traditions, or rituals. If you have to go for counseling to get to a point where you can talk calmly about the subject, do it.

2. Do research: You need to know enough about each other's beliefs, religious background, and the options available to be able to reach a mutually satisfactory solution. Talk to each other, to your families, if possible, and to clergy to get as much information as you can. Find the most tolerant, knowledgeable, and supportive people you can to talk to, and have them explain their point of view about it. You don't have to agree with your partner to understand what he or she is thinking.

3. Give yourselves time: Don't insist that you have to make this decision right now. The more time you can spend understanding the issues and developing options, the more likely you'll come up with a solution both of you can accept. No matter how long you waited to discuss this, or how long you've been struggling about it, you still don't have to decide it in a rush.

4. Talk about it repeatedly: Talk to other couples, to clergy, to friends, and to family several times to create more understanding and brainstorm about options. If you can find other couples who have resolved religious differences, find out what they decided.

5. Explain your partner's point of view: When talking about it to each other, or to someone else who is supportive, explain each other's point of view, which will help you understand.

6. Focus on your children: Keep your focus on what would be best for your children, and if they are old enough to understand, bring them into the discussion. Don't try to persuade them to either side, but present the options as objectively as you can and find out what your children think about it.

7. Experiment: Be willing to try some experiments. You could devote every other week to each religion, for example, reading books on each other's faith or belief, and so on. Jan and Ron tried living Jewish traditions the first and third weeks of the month and Catholic traditions on the second and fourth weeks.

Jan says, "I had known of Shabbat observances, lighting the candles and observing sundown Friday to sundown Saturday as the Sabbath, but I never really experienced the beauty and grace, and the honor given to the mother of the household. Synagogue services on Friday night were a lovely way to end the week, and I truly felt the blessing of lighting the Shabbat candles. Of course, I've enjoyed Jewish-style food and had already learned how to make Ron's favorites from his mother. His family doesn't keep strict kosher, so I was relieved not to have to manage that. "Ron says: "I found that Catholic candle lighting felt familiar, and loved the beauty of the small Catholic Church we attended. On the other hand, I was pretty uncomfortable with some of the words of the Mass. For Jan's family, their religious observances and feelings seem to be separate from their Italian heritage, and the foods they eat. They don't seem to connect it up as much. In my family, eating pastrami or brisket is Jewish, but they don't see eating spaghetti in the same way. To them, the food is Italian, not Catholic."

8. Create a blend of your own: Whether you realize it or not, within the doctrine, liturgy, and beliefs of every religion, people are picking and choosing. You can belong to a neighborhood church that is Presbyterian, for example, and find another Presbyterian church down the street handling things in a different way. Of course, the differences between two different faiths or beliefs will probably be much greater, but you can still adapt the tenets of your different beliefs in a way that will work for both of you. If you could be flexible and tolerant enough to marry someone of a different faith, you can be flexible enough to develop a blend of both beliefs that will be workable.

> Learning about each other's religion by practicing forms of it in their experiment helped Jan and Ron decide to have a candle-lighting ceremony with prayers in English on Friday nights and to say grace at every meal. They've decided to wait until their children grow older and let the family decide as a unit which religious schooling they'll give them. "Ron and I want them to be old enough to think before we indoctrinate them with religion. We'll teach them about God, and why it's important to be loving and not selfish or mean, and we'll observe traditions from both our families, but we'll let the specific religious information wait. We've decided to permit their grandparents to take them to services or teach them observances as they choose, as long as they aren't critical or negative about the other faith.

9. Avoid right/wrong discussions: As I've mentioned before, arguing about who is right or wrong will not solve anything. Instead, work on understanding what is important to each of you, then find a way to incorporate that and resolve your differences. Focus on the problem only long enough to understand what it is, then switch the focus of your discussion to what will work and what will solve the problem in such a way that both of you can live with your mutual decision.

STRUGGLE
Blended Families and Stepparenting

No situation lends itself to arguments and bitterness more than stepfamilies, or blended families. Not only do you have to contend with the differences between you and your spouse about child rearing; but also your stepchildren may have other parents who differ with your decisions. Some or all of the children in your family may be commuting back and forth between parents and, in addition, might be upset by whatever happened to split up their biological parents.

Helen says, "We have three children. Bethany is nine years old and my daughter with my ex-husband. Laurie is six years old, and Karen is twenty-three months (will be two years old in November). Laurie and Karen are my children with George. He plays the mind games with Bethany the most, and I want to protect her because she is my daughter from another man. George has started to play the mind games with Laurie because she is getting older. He often tells them, "If you don't do this, you're going to get spanked." But, I see the fear in my children, especially in Bethany's eyes. George doesn't understand that the anticipation of the punishment is much worse than the actual punishment, especially when he may not follow it up with any punishment at all. I would look at Bethany when things like this are going on and her eyes would say, 'Mom, save me.' That's why I feel the need to save her. Bethany's father doesn't threaten to hit her; he and I used to just give her time-outs or take away privileges."

"We fight a lot about this, but not in front of the kids. Once we were arguing about his mind games and I stormed out of the house and left him with the kids for six hours. I went to my mother's house to cool off."

George says: "I don't think I'm any harder on Bethany than on my own two kids. In my family, we were actually spanked with a belt. I'm not spanking anyone. I don't think the girls are afraid of me, and I think Helen is too protective. The girls need to know they'll be punished, or they won't behave. But, I don't think the fights Helen and I are having are helping anything."

SITUATION

Different Styles

Helen and George have basic differences about parenting their daughters, made more complicated by the stepfamily dynamic. They need to find a way to agree. Disagreements about discipline and punishment are common. Ideally, single adults with children should talk about the issues of co-parenting and blending a family before they try it, but few really talk seriously. As we discussed earlier in this chapter, raising children together involves values, parenting and discipline styles, and religion and ethnic traditions, which must be understood and agreed upon by the parents. Single parents should never rush into marriage before they've worked out their parenting, discipline, household rules, finances, and so on. The most important thing is to give the various relationships time. If you're not of one accord, your children will use it to "divide and conquer"—to the detriment of everyone, including themselves. Once you've done the deed and created a blended family, you'll have to work through anything that didn't get handled before. Differences in parenting styles are exaggerated because parenting began before you got together, and there are exes involved who have their own ideas of how you should parent their children, too. Things can get even more complicated when children are sharing time between parents. Your stepchildren will challenge your authority, but don't forget they do this with their birth parents, too.

SOLUTION

Family Meetings and Transitions

Blended families can be a challenge, but I also have many adults in my practice who say a caring, helpful stepparent was the best thing that happened to them. You already have been given tools to accomplish most of these things.

As discussed above, differences in parenting styles can be resolved by taking parenting classes to learn some new options. Many classes are offered, especially for blended families. It's critical not to get into struggles with the children's other parents. Even if you disagree about how things are handled at the other parent's house, it's more important that you find a way to agree about parenting in your house than trying to control other places and people.

In addition to all the techniques discussed earlier in this chapter, there are two techniques that can help stepfamilies overcome difficulties and create a bond as a new family.

Technique #1: Family Meetings

I highly recommend every family, including stepfamilies, to have family meetings (that include everyone) on a weekly basis. Children should also be involved in making decisions. When the children feel they've been heard, they'll be less resistant to family rules. If the children have a say in devising reasonable punishments for infractions, they'll feel the rules are fair. Consistency is important, and so is setting boundaries. Change is difficult for everyone, so understand that it will take a while for things to settle down. If you're loving, available as much as possible, and consistent about enforcing the rules, and each child has some special recognition for his or her activities, talents, and needs, your new blended family will work smoothly. Every member of your family has a right to have his or her opinions respected. You don't have to agree or go along with what your child wants, but you should at least know what it is, and your child should know why you're overriding his or her preferences. Regular family meetings where everyone, including the children, expresses feelings, negative and positive, and all of you work together to solve problems, can help a lot.

Guidelines for Family Meetings

Begin family meetings as soon as possible, whether you think you have any issues to discuss or not. Choose a time when everyone can get together weekly, and suggest to everyone that you order take-out food or cook something easy that everyone enjoys.

Sit down on a weekly basis with your family, and discuss everything about your relationship, positive and problematic, and how it's going for each of you. If you have small children, include them and get their input, also.

Begin the session with a brief prayer, affirmation, or blessing, and a round of compliments, where each member gives a small tribute to every other member to create a positive atmosphere.

At the meeting, everyone (parents and children who are old enough to talk) can go through the following three steps:

1. State three good things about others in the family.
2. Mention one thing to be improved and what to do to make it better. Small children will need help until they understand, but they will catch on quickly. Even you and one child can do this.
3. State whatever problems or concerns the person has. Everyone can work together to come up with a solution. The only thing that should not happen at these meetings is criticism and complaining. State a problem, if you have one, in matter-of-fact terms, and use "I" messages: "I don't like it when the house gets messy," "I have a problem at school," "I don't want to argue with Susie anymore."

This simple meeting will do more for the state of your intimate relationship than you can imagine. Given a chance, and the right atmosphere, most problems can be solved before they become disasters.

Technique #2: Transitions—Handling Different Rules in Different Houses

Blended families also often have to deal with shared custody, with various children leaving at different times to spend time with the other birth parent. These changes require "re-entry" discussions and rituals, so everyone can adjust each time.

What if your ex's, grandma's, or child care provider's rules are different from your house rules? Children can quickly learn that the rules in another house they spend time in are different from yours. Think about what the rules are in your house, and have a "re-entry" discussion each time your children come home and each time they leave. Talk with them about what's different between here and their other parent's house, and give them a chance to make the transition. Don't set yourself up in opposition to the other parent, just let the children know the rules are different at your house, and in what way they differ. When you give your children a little help in making their transitions back and forth, you'll find that it's less of a struggle to resume smooth family life.

Chapter 5

SOLVING OTHER STRUGGLES

In the first four chapters, we explored the major reasons couples fight over money, sex, and kids, and some basic solutions. Of course, there are many other possible reasons you and your spouse could be fighting. The good news is that the solution to all square-offs, no matter what they are about, is to learn to negotiate rather than argue. The bad news is that learning to talk rather than fight requires change in how you're thinking about the discussion, and how you're talking to each other.

It's not reasonable to expect that you'll never argue in your marriage. Instead, the goal of this book is to minimize the number of fights you have and teach you how to fight without damaging your relationship.

Dirk, a thirty-five-year-old electrical contractor, and Cheryl, a twenty-eight-year-old receptionist, are a couple who have only been married for two years. Now their honeymoon phase is over, and they're quarreling about household chores. Cheryl wants to talk to Dirk about how they divide up household chores; she feels overloaded. But every time she tries, he puts her off. If she insists, he gets angry and defensive, and before she knows it, they're fighting and the issue never gets discussed. Cheryl feels that Dirk always "wins"—and she never gets a chance to state her side of the issue. Dirk complains that she doesn't respond to him sexually any more. Even if Dirk (the "winner") feels good about getting what he wants, there are unpleasant repercussions later when Cheryl's (the "loser") anger and resentment build up until they erupt in sexual withholding, rage, depression, or separation.

Power Struggles

Like Dirk and Cheryl, you may feel that solving relationship problems has always meant a struggle in which you or your partner may "win" the specific issue but both of you end up unsatisfied and sometimes resentful. All your attempts at negotiation seem to end up in the same old outcome:

- *Guilt and obligation:* When one partner uses guilt or obligation to coerce the other into doing something, it may work in the short run but have an unpleasant aftermath. Using phrases like "if you loved me, you'd . . ." or "how can you do that to me (expect that of me, not do that for me)," is a way of trying to get something by making the other person feel guilty. Just asking directly for what you want— "Please help me with the dishes"—will work much better, and not create more problems later.
- *Threats and emotional blackmail:* When one partner won't take no for an answer, his or her requests become demands, and this creates resistance from the second partner, then the first applies pressure (which can be tears, hysteria, or rage) and threats until the second partner gives in, then the cycle repeats. This may begin harmlessly and then escalate until it's very overbearing and abusive. It is the opposite of guilt. Rather than saying "If you loved me . . ." the attitude here is "If you don't do what I want, I won't love you."
- *Courtroom logic:* One partner attempts to prove a "case," that he or she is "right," and deserves to get what he or she wants. It is a relentless argument, lawyer-style, which

sounds very logical, but it is completely one-sided and does not take the other partner's wants, feelings, and needs into account. In fact, it often belittles or "logically" dismisses them.

- *Keeping the peace:* Passive partners try to be "nice" and give in to the above manipulations to "keep the peace" by never saying what they want for fear it will "upset" their partner.
- *Compromising:* Marriage manuals often recommend solutions in which one or both partners give up some of what they want in order to reach agreement. It is a time-honored "best" way to solve problems, but couples who do it usually find that resentment builds as they give up what they want bit by bit.
- *Hammering away:* This is relentless persistence without gentleness or consideration for the other's wants, often called "nagging," "badgering," or "harassment." One partner just keeps insisting on getting what he or she wants until the other gives in.

If you have a history of power struggles, negotiations can be stalled because your partner is suspicious that the offer to talk is really an attempt to manipulate.

Cheryl: Dirk, I want to talk to you about the household chores.

Dirk: Oh, honey, not right now, I'm tired from work, and I want to watch this movie.

—later—

Cheryl: Dirk, your movie's over, can we talk now?

Dirk: I've got all this work I brought home. Can't it wait?

Cheryl, knowing that the next step leads to an argument, gives up, but feels angry at Dirk. She's silent and cold the rest of the evening.

Dirk is avoiding Cheryl in the fear that the discussion will be just another power struggle; someone is going to lose, someone will end up feeling bad, or nobody will win. Worse yet, after all the hassle, frustration, and resentment, the problem could still be unsolved. So when she wants to talk, his response is "Not now," because he's really thinking, "Why bother?"

In the dialogue that follows, you'll see how, with some practice, Cheryl and Dirk learned to reassure each other, fight fair, and overcome their old habit of struggling.

Reluctance or refusal to discuss an issue is usually the result of one or more specific fears, such as:

- Fear of being manipulated or overpowered
- Fear of being taken advantage of, made a fool of, or "conned"
- Fear of having another fight
- Fear that the discussion will be a long, complicated hassle (hard work) without a worthwhile result (a waste of time)
- Fear of losing, or having to give up something important
- Fear that talking won't go well or work at all

Each of these fears, and any others that might come up, can be discovered, communicated, and eased, which will undermine your partner's resistance to discussion.

Guidelines for Reassurance

Find out what your partner's fears are. If your partner won't talk with you, and you suspect he or she may be afraid of a bad outcome or wishing to avoid a power struggle, *don't just assume you know that to be true*. Guessing will confuse both of you and increase your partner's resistance. Instead follow these steps to determine your partner's fear:

1. Tell your partner what you observe that leads you to believe he or she is avoiding dealing with the problem. ("We agreed to take turns taking out the garbage, and you haven't done your share." "When I ask you to negotiate, you say you're busy.")

2. Because you can sound like you're complaining or nagging, be sure you let your partner know that you're just explaining what leads you to believe he or she doesn't want to negotiate. Ask your partner if what you see is correct and if it does mean he or she is reluctant to negotiate.

3. If your partner denies that he or she is reluctant, ask again if the two of you can discuss the problem, since your partner says there is no reason not to.

4. If your partner then acknowledges (admits) that he or she is reluctant, let your partner know that you care about these feelings of reluctance by asking why. Whatever your partner says, don't argue about it. Listen to the answers carefully and repeat what he or she says to make it clear that you heard and understood.

If your partner has trouble figuring out what causes his or her reluctance, offer to read the above list of fears together to see what fits. To help keep a cooperative atmosphere (and counteract the feeling that only one of you has, or is, a problem) acknowledge your own fears (as well as your partner's) as you read the list. To get fears into the open where they can be put to rest, it is often helpful to consider what the worst possible outcome of agreeing to negotiate could be and allow your imagination to run wild. (What if you find out you're incompatible and you have to break up? What if you get into such a bad fight you don't talk for days?) If either of you are having such scary thoughts, it's better you get them into the open where you can figure out how to handle those unlikely events if they do happen.

Here's how Cheryl learned to use these guidelines (informally) in response to Dirk.

Cheryl (*offers to negotiate*): Will you work this household maintenance problem out with me?

Dirk (*avoids issue*): Maybe later. I'm reading right now.

Cheryl (*lets Dirk know what she thinks is happening*): Dirk, I've invited you several times to work this out, and I think you're avoiding it. Will you tell me why you keep putting me off?

Dirk (*begins to express fear*): I don't want to get into it. Why should I? If I say no, you won't drop it. If we talk about it, we'll just fight. I won't get anything I want.

Cheryl (*acknowledges fear by paraphrasing it, with active listening*): You think I'm going to nag you to make you do chores you don't want to do?

Dirk (*relaxes a little, less defensive*): Yes. You've tried it before.

Cheryl (*more acknowledgment*): You're right, I guess I have nagged you before. And now you're afraid I'm going to try it again?

Dirk: Yes.

Cheryl is clear now that the problem is Dirk's fear (from past experience) that Cheryl will nag him. Now she knows what to reassure Dirk about.

Reassure Your Partner

Avoiding a power struggle is avoiding something unpleasant. If Cheryl can reassure Dirk that the discussion itself will not be unpleasant and it won't lead to something unpleasant, he will have nothing to fear, and reassurance will smooth the way. If she can show him she won't overpower him by nagging, he'll be more likely to give up his power struggle.

Cheryl began by listening to Dirk's fears. Now she can reassure him effectively. They can figure out together how they would handle the situation if any of their worst fears came true ("If the argument got so bad we weren't talking, we could see a counselor"). Knowing that you have a strategy to take care of yourselves if things don't go right will give Dirk the additional confidence to try negotiating. If any of your partner's fears are based on things that have happened before, acknowledge that it did happen, and explain what is different now ("You're right, I did nag before, but I've realized that doesn't work, and I want to change that").

Once you get more accustomed to reassuring your partner, it can be done much more informally, as Cheryl reassures Dirk in the rest of their discussion.

Cheryl (*more acknowledgment*): You're right, I guess I have nagged you before. And now you're afraid I'm going to try it again?

Dirk: Yes.

Cheryl (*acknowledging and reassuring Dirk's fear*): I can understand how you'd think I would nag you into doing what I want, I've done that before over different issues. I know I've used anger, silence, and coldness to win arguments before. But now I've learned some new things, and I realize that my old ways of winning have damaged the relationship. I want to work together to come up with a solution we both like.

Dirk (*still afraid*): Yeah, but what if I don't like the solution?

Cheryl (*reassures again*): Then we keep working on it until we have a solution we both like.

Dirk (*not sure*): Sounds too good to be true.

Cheryl (*acknowledging, reassuring*): I know. But I think it's worth a try. We won't agree on anything that doesn't suit us both, and if we can't do it, we'll be no worse off than we are now.

Dirk (*one last fear*): Are you setting me up?

Cheryl (*one more reassurance*): No. I really want you to be happy with our solution. Will you give me a chance to show you by discussing housekeeping with me?

Dirk (*agrees, with reservations*): OK, but if you harp at me or nag me, I'm quitting.

Cheryl: OK, it's a deal.

As you practice reassuring yourself and your partner, you'll find it gets easier to do, and the more reassurance you give each other, the easier and smoother your negotiation will be.

Arguments Over "Nothing"

As I said in chapter 1, couples' fights are often symbolic—you can argue over petty little things when you're actually angry about something else—usually about sex, power, or abandonment issues. Women are more likely to get angry for emotional reasons (jealousy, neglect). Men often get angry about money and lack of sex. Often people enter marriage with a store of anger left over from earlier relationships and childhood, which can be really confusing to both parties.

You may have heard the adage, "Don't let the sun set on an argument" or "never go to bed angry," but often letting things go for a few hours or one day will give you both a chance to calm down and see things more rationally. If you're trying to discuss a problem and you keep arguing and not getting anywhere, it's better to take a time-out and come back to it later.

To reduce the stress of a problem, discuss with your spouse what you do and do not want, because unmet expectations lead to disappointment and anger. Once you are clear with each other, you'll be much more able to make a mutually satisfactory decision. Make a habit of having this discussion before facing important decisions.

Anger

Anger is the force within us that rises when something needs to change. If we act on the need to create change, the anger can be channeled effectively, but if it's not redirected to something effective, the frustration will build, leading to rage. Anger that is allowed to get out of control is as destructive as a hurricane, but anger that is expressed in healthy ways can "clear the air," just as a storm does. The aftermath of a healthy, not too violent storm allows us to appreciate the pleasures of calmness.

People who have angry outbursts, whether at spouses or freeway traffic, have poor impulse control. They are often "stuck" in the early temper-tantrum stage (about age two and a half to three) because they never learned to manage their own anger. Whoever was supposed to help them manage their temper, such as parents or teachers, were absent, intimidated, or helpless, and they allowed the child to grow into a raging adult. They may also have witnessed a family member who was a "rageaholic" and frequently angry or violent. People who rage don't know how to do "emotional maintenance" and shake off stress. They also don't know how to quit when something is getting to them. Those who allow themselves to rage don't know how to tell they're on the brink, or how to stop. They often have a sense of entitlement ("I just have a bad temper"— said with some pride) and a lack of emotional maturity. They're actually like emotional three-year-olds in adult bodies, which is dangerous.

The difference between people who lose their temper (throw fits, throw objects, scream and yell) and those who don't is that those with self-control can feel that they're getting upset, getting close to "losing it." With enough harassment and pressure, anyone can be goaded into rage.

People who keep control of their anger just stop or leave the situation earlier—before they are pushed so far. They respect their own anger and deal with it effectively. As soon as they feel anger is getting out of control, they stop what they're doing, walk away, change their thinking/attitude, write in a journal, pray, or call a friend to get calmed down.

Anger management is not difficult once the angry person "gets" that just spewing your anger about is not healthy or right. Most angry people have a feeling of entitlement—"I can't change who I am"—that prevents them from wanting to control their anger. Once they understand that losing one's temper doesn't accomplish anything, ruins relationships, and makes them look weak, not strong, then learning to control anger is not hard.

You Have Choices

To solve your anger problems, make some choices: Do you want to keep doing what you're doing, or do you want to learn self-control and have a life that works? Do you want to look good to your peers, or do you want to be successful? Do you want to be right, or be loved? In every case, learning to control your anger and act responsibly will get you more of what you want from life.

If you or your partner tends to get loud and obnoxious frequently, it's a bigger problem than just struggling. Perhaps you need to swear off drinking or get some therapy. No matter what, you must find a way to end this childish and demeaning behavior. If your partner tends to be too argumentative, use behavioral training: Treat your partner very well as long as he or she is agreeable and will discuss things calmly. If your spouse gets oppositional and controlling, try being silent. Do not respond at all. If your partner doesn't stop after a few moments, or if she or he gets louder, that may be evidence of anger management problems. Out-of-control yelling and bad behavior is actually a childish temper tantrum, and it is not necessary to put up with it. Leave on the spot. If you're home, go to another room, or take a walk. If you're dining out, take a taxi, leave money for the bill if there is one, but get out of there. It doesn't matter how important the occasion is; it's ruined anyway. Once your mate realizes you're not going to put up with bad behavior, he or she may come to understand it is unacceptable and change it if possible, or perhaps even get necessary therapy.

The person who loses his or her temper looks like the bad guy to everyone else, no matter who started the problem, or who is really at fault. Keeping your cool is a very important social skill. It doesn't matter who's right, who started it, or whether it's fair. He (or she) who "loses it" to win an argument actually loses everything instead.

To get better at controlling your anger, use the following exercise to visualize a scene where you got angry, and replay the tape several times, to get a clear picture of yourself responding in different ways. When you do this, you are actually rehearsing different reactions, and giving yourself new options. You always have choices: laugh, walk away, get thoughtful, be afraid, be angry, or be reasonable.

EXERCISE: Rewinding the Tape

1. Imagine a previous angry situation as if it's occurring now. Get as clear a picture of the scene as possible, imagining what people are wearing, what the room looks like, and so on.

2. Mentally play the scene as if it's a video, and see how it develops. Don't worry if it plays out according to your worst fears; just watch it as you would any video.

3. Because this scene didn't go well originally, consider what you'd like to change about what you're doing (remember, you can't control the others in the scene, but you can get them to respond differently by giving them something different to respond to). Rewind and replay this mental image, trying new ways to handle it until you are successful (that is, you handle the situation without losing your temper).

4. Play the tape a few more times with this successful process and outcome until you feel confident you can do and say what you are visualizing.

5. Play the tape again and again, visualizing your successful outcome. The more you replay it and practice your new responses, the easier it will be to access them in the next discussion.

6. You have just reprogrammed your mind to create some new responses to tense or angry situations, and you'll find these responses are available to you when you need them. Use this technique any time you're concerned about an upcoming discussion or confrontation.

If your partner's anger is not that bad, but you tend to obsess about it and have a hard time forgiving small slights, you can use the following technique.

How to Let Go of Small Things
1. Viewpoint: Take a mental step back and look at this from a bigger view. In the context of your whole life, how important is this? Is it more important than your happiness and good opinion of yourself? Most of the time you won't think so.

2. Self-understanding: If someone or something upsets you, don't exacerbate the problem by getting on your own case for reacting. Reactions are normal—it's what we do with them that counts.

3. Rise above: Don't allow yourself to be drawn down into someone else's negativity. Instead, use the power of your personality to come out of this situation with a better result.

4. Benefit of the doubt: After your partner or someone else hurts your feelings, acknowledge that you're feeling bad, then consider that the other person is probably more clumsy than intentionally hurtful. The world is full of emotional klutzes who don't realize the impact of their words and actions, and they create more problems for themselves than for you.

5. Consider the source: If your partner is under a lot of stress, consider what must be going on inside that person's head and be grateful that you're not in his or her shoes. When someone is ill, grieving, or worried, they're liable to speak without thinking and say something crabby. As long as it's a temporary and infrequent problem, you can forgive it.

Fighting about Other People

Dorothy and Bill, the twenty-something executives who solved their money struggles in chapter 2, and who grew up in similar, lower-income families with hardworking parents, are struggling over their respective families:

Bill is frustrated: "Dorothy doesn't care at all about my family. She is jealous and resentful about my mother, and she hates my brother. She always wants to go to her parents for Thanksgiving dinner. My family would like to see us, too."

"Bill doesn't give me any credit for how far out of my way I go to get along with his family," says Dorothy. "My family loves him, and they all get along fine, but his family has always been cold and hostile toward me. I see them any other time he wants to, and I don't complain. Why should I want to spend my holidays with them, when we have so much fun at my parents?

"I guess Bill's right, I don't like his family and I don't like to go over there. We've been married five years, and they still treat me like some stranger Bill brought in unexpectedly. I buy the Christmas presents for Bill's family, and make sure they all say they're from both of us, but most of their presents are for him—I always feel left out. They are always talking about when they were little, which leaves me out of the conversation. They even talk about Bill's old girlfriends.

"I've tried everything I can think of to be friendly to them, but now I've had it. My family makes Bill welcome, they talk to him and we all play cards together when we go over there. I know he likes my folks, and they like him. They give him presents at Christmas, and they treat him like a son. Except for some pressure about when we're going to have children, our time with them is always nice, and I know Bill likes it. He could talk to his family about the way they treat me, but he won't."

"Dorothy's right about my family," says Bill. "They have never been very good about letting outsiders in, my brother's girlfriend notices it, too. But they're still my family, and I want to spend some holiday time with them. Why does Dorothy have to take their casual attitude toward her so personally? Would it kill her to spend a couple of days a year over there?

"I wish my family were more like Dorothy's. They're neat. We do have fun over there, and I like her parents a lot. When we do decide to have kids, they'll be great grandparents, so I can see why they're anxious, and it doesn't bother me. I think they're great in-laws, and I have a good time with them, but I still want to spend some of our time with my family. I don't want to have to choose between Dorothy and my family, or between Dorothy's family and my own. I feel like Rodney King, pleading 'Can't we all just get along?'

"I feel uncomfortable about telling my family to be nicer to Dorothy. First of all, I don't think it would help—they'd just decide I was making trouble. Secondly, it would create hard feelings. I just want Dorothy to go see them because they're my family."

Dorothy and Bill actually agree about the differences between their families—their arguments are about how to handle visiting, and what's fair. They need to sit down together and work out a deal that works for both of them. Even if Bill's family doesn't know how to include Dorothy,

Bill can help her feel included, or maybe he can go to occasions at his family by himself while Dorothy goes out with friends or just takes some alone time. Alternatively, they could go to Bill's family for a brief time and take separate cars so she can make an excuse and leave earlier than he does. It might even be helpful for Bill and his brother to talk to the rest of the family about how they make Dorothy and the brother's girlfriend feel left out. If Dorothy and Bill are willing to consider enough options, they'll find a solution they can both agree on.

One way to handle difficult family members is to treat them as members of someone else's family—that is, be polite and a little distant, but pleasant. If you were with a friend's family, and someone did something odd or slightly rude or they excluded you, you'd basically ignore it and just politely sit through what they're doing or saying, maintaining a pleasant demeanor. You can decide you don't like them, but you don't need to let it show.

Family members can also butt in and become involved in your arguments, making everything more difficult. If you first get clear with each other about an issue such as with whom to spend the holidays, then let others who may be involved know your decision, you'll present a united front. No matter what is happening, if you take the time to think, you'll be able to come up with several options, and you won't allow other people's expectations to add to the stress.

For example, if you have an uncle who gets drunk at holidays and makes passes at the women, uses profanity, or otherwise behaves badly, you can figure out how to handle him in advance. Identify extended family members or friends who might be problems so you can make agreements about how to defuse them before they create problems. In the case of the inebriated uncle, for example, if you know what time he tends to get obnoxious (these behaviors usually fit a pattern), you can decide to come early, while he's still behaving well, or much later, after he's passed out. Or you can let your uncle and the rest of the family know that his behavior is unacceptable to you, and you'll reserve the right to leave whenever he gets too difficult.

The best way to handle anyone who's difficult, whether it's a family member, friend of a friend, or co-worker; is to give the problem person an "adult time-out."

Adult Time-Out

Whenever someone you know behaves badly in your presence, giving that adult a "time-out" is a powerful and subtle way of fixing the problem. Modern parents use a time-out to discipline small children. The child is sent to a corner, or a room, to think about his or her behavior. While you can't really discipline an adult so visibly, you can accomplish the same result in a more subtle way. An adult variation of the time-out works on anyone—in your family, at work, at school, or among your friends—who is acting childish or misbehaving. All you need to do is become very distant and polite around the person who is not treating you well. No personal talk and interaction, no joking, no emotion. Be very polite so the person cannot accuse you of being unpleasant, mean, or rude. There is no need to explain what you are doing; the problem person will get the message from your behavior—which is much more effective. If you've never tried this, you'll be amazed at how effective becoming polite and pleasant but distant can be. Most of the time, the other person's behavior will immediately become more subdued around you, and often, much more caring. Eventually, that person may ask you what's wrong or why you've changed, and at that point (and only at that point) you have an opportunity to tell him or her what the problem behavior is, and why you don't like it. Learning to put obnoxious people in time-outs right at the beginning of unpleasant behavior can make it unnecessary to use tougher tactics at all. And if the person's behavior doesn't change, you can leave him or her in "time-out" and you'll be protected from it.

Bonus Guidelines: Attentive Speaking

No matter when you're talking to other members of your family, your children, or your spouse, using attentive speaking will help you make sure you're communicating.

The average person pays more attention to what she's saying or thinking about than what she is hearing or how her words are "landing" on the other person. This self-involvement gets worse during an argument. You can become a much more effective communicator by using attentive speaking. This is a simple and highly effective technique that will help you pay attention to how well you're communicating, whether it's with your partner, children, extended family, or co-workers.

Attentive speaking simply means paying attention, not only to what you are saying, but also to how your partner is receiving it. If you watch carefully your partner's facial expression, body movements, and posture (looking interested, fidgeting, looking bored, eyes wandering, attempting to interrupt, facial expressions of anger or confusion, or a blank stare) when you want to get a point across, all will provide clues to help you know whether you are being understood. By using the following guidelines, you can learn to observe your partner as he or she is listening to you and see whether you are successfully communicating what you want your partner to hear, without any verbal communication from your partner. This is especially effective if your partner:

- Is not very talkative
- Thinks disagreeing, or objecting will "hurt your feelings"

- Is the unemotional, strong, silent type
- Is easily overwhelmed in a discussion
- Is passive, depressed, or withdrawn

Sometimes, such partners are reluctant to let you know if they have a negative reaction to what you are saying. If your partner is not receiving what you are saying as you intended, and you persist in talking without finding out your partner's feelings, he or she could become more and more upset by what you are saying, stop listening, get very confused, mentally object or silently argue with you, or not want to be talked to at all. If you don't use attentive speaking to see the clues, you can be chattering blithely along and suddenly your partner will react with anger, misunderstand you, or just not be interested in listening anymore, and all your efforts to communicate are wasted. By using the guidelines that follow, you can figure out when you aren't communicating well or getting the reaction you want.

Using attentive speaking will help you:

- Avoid overwhelming your partner with too much information at once (because you will notice when he or she looks overwhelmed, bored, or distracted)
- Keep your partner's interest in what you have to say (by teaching you how to ask a question when you see your partner's attention slipping away)
- Understand when what you say is misunderstood (by observing facial expressions and noticing when they're different from what you expect)
- Gauge your partner's reaction when he or she doesn't say anything (by facial expressions, body language, and attentiveness)
- Tell when your partner is too distracted, stressed, or upset to really hear what you're saying (by facial expressions, body language, and attentiveness)

The following steps will help you learn to speak attentively.

1. Watch your listener. When it is important to you to communicate effectively, be careful not to get so engrossed in what you are saying that you forget to watch your partner. Keep your eyes on your partner's face and body, which will let your partner know you care about whether he or she hears you, increase your partner's tendency to make eye contact with you, and therefore cause him or her to listen more carefully.

2. Look for clues in your partner's facial expression and body position. Does your partner have a smile, a frown, a glassy-eyed stare? Is he or she upright and alert, slumped and sullen, turned away from you and inattentive? Also observe your partner's movements (leaning toward you, pulling away from you, fidgeting, restlessness). For example, if you say "I love you," and you observe that your partner turns away and looks out the window, you are getting clues that you weren't received the way you wanted to be. Either your partner is too distracted to hear you, or he or she is having a problem with what you said.

3. Ask, don't guess. If you get a response that seems unusual or inappropriate to what you said (you think you're giving a compliment and your partner looks confused, hurt, or angry; or you think you're stating objective facts and your partner looks like he or she disagrees; you're angry, but your partner is smiling), ask a gentle question. For example, "I thought I was giving you a compliment, but you look annoyed. Did I say something wrong?" Or, "Gee, I thought you'd be happy to hear this but you look upset. Please tell me what you're thinking." Or, "I'm angry about what you just said, but you're smiling. Did I misunderstand you?" Or, just "Do you agree?"

4. Don't talk too long. If your partner becomes fidgety or looks off into space as you talk, either what you're saying is emotionally uncomfortable, the time is not good for talking (business pressures, stress, the ball game is on), your partner is bored, or you've been talking too long.

If you think you've been talking too long or your partner is bored, invite him or her to comment: "What do you think?" or "Do you see it the same way?" or perhaps "Am I talking too much (or too fast)?" If you think it's a bad time, just ask: "You look distracted. Is this a good time to talk about this?" If it is a bad time, then try again at a different time.

5. Look for confusion. When you're paying attention as you speak, incomprehension and confusion are also easy to spot. If your partner begins to have a blank or glassy-eyed look, or looks worried or confused, you may be putting out too many ideas all at once, or you may not be explaining your thoughts clearly enough. Again, ask a question: "Am I making sense to you?" "Am I going too fast?" or, "Do you have any questions?" Sometimes, just a pause in what you are saying will give your partner the room to ask a question and get his or her confusion cleared up.

6. Don't blame. Blaming your listener—for example, by insisting that he or she just isn't paying enough attention—will only exacerbate the problem. Instead, ask a question, such as "I don't think I'm explaining this clearly. Have I lost you?" Or, "Am I bringing up too many things at once?" Phrasing the questions to show that you're looking for ways to improve your style and clarity invites cooperation and encourages teamwork.

By using the above guidelines, you can find out immediately, as you are speaking, if you are communicating well with your partner. If you see signs of confusion or trouble, you can put things back on track quite easily, whether you're speaking to your partner, a child, or anyone else.

When you and your partner know how to hear and understand each other, you'll find that any struggle can be solved. No matter what the issue is, it is never more important than keeping your partnership healthy and productive. As long as the two of you are a functioning team that can work together to solve problems and resolve issues, you'll be able to deal with whatever comes along as the years go by. In the next chapter, you'll learn more about the habit of fighting, how to overcome it, and how to defuse the myths and expectations that you may have which make struggling seem necessary.

Chapter 6

FIGHTING FAIR

In the previous chapters, you've learned how to effectively communicate and solve the three major couple problems without fighting. But you may find it's not so easy to give up your struggles. One of the reasons you may have trouble letting go of the fighting habit is social expectations (expectations other people have about marriage) and myths (common beliefs not based on fact).

Myths and Expectations about Fighting

There are many myths and expectations about fighting in marriage. Couples come into my office frequently believing that fighting is a necessary part of being a couple. Hanging on to these ideas makes it difficult to let go of fighting.

Some of the most prevalent myths about fighting are:

Myth #1: Fighting clears the air and brings out the truth. Fighting is not necessary to "clear the air." Getting heated up does not make you tell truths you wouldn't tell otherwise. What happens when couples fight and get emotional is that both parties say things they don't mean, or they say them in much nastier ways than is really true. It is possible to discuss anything that is or is not happening between you in a calm and logical manner that will lead to more truth telling and air clearing than fighting and arguing will ever accomplish.

Myth #2: Within your family it's OK to "let it all hang out"—to be as emotional as you want and say things you'd never say to a friend or a boss. Whether you're fighting or not (or drunk, or upset), you're still responsible for everything you say and do. The hurtful, mean, and outrageous things you say will be remembered by your spouse or other family members who hear them.

Myth #3: Fighting just happens; you can't control it. You always have a choice about your behavior and how you express yourself. If you've developed a fighting habit or never learned to control your temper, you may need to do some work, but you can learn to behave differently.

Myth #4: My wife (or husband) makes me do it. She (he) yells first. No one else is responsible for your behavior. You are not responsible for anyone else's words or actions. You can *always* choose not to yell back, to speak calmly, or to leave the room. Your partner cannot fight alone.

Myth #5: Any time we get angry, it's natural to argue and yell. Arguing and shouting are not the only ways to express your anger. They're just the most dramatic ways. As a matter of fact, they're the least effective ways to reach a solution for whatever is making you angry.

Myth #6: It's a family trait—everyone in my family argues. Fighting, temper tantrums, and arguing may be common in your original family, but it's not genetic, inherited, or inevitable. It's still learned behavior, and it's a dysfunctional family trait. It's a habit, and you can overcome it for the benefit of your spouse and children.

Myth #7: It's OK to yell, shout, curse, throw things, and hit walls as long as I don't hit a person. These raging behaviors are classified as emotional abuse, which is just as damaging to families as physical abuse. Evidence of emotional abuse is enough to have your children detained by Child Protective Services in many states. If a problem is reported and the police arrive to witness the behavior, it can even cause a raging spouse to be hauled off in handcuffs. I tell clients who are behaving this way to separate until they get their anger under control, which requires anger management classes or therapy. If this is happening in your house, it must be stopped now. Skip down to the Domestic Violence section in this chapter for specific instructions on how to keep yourself and your family safe.

Harmful Fighting Styles, and What to Do

Some kinds of fights are particularly destructive and damaging to the people involved, and the habit of fighting itself is counterproductive. Each fight you're willing to have will further ingrain your habit of fighting. I forbid my client couples to fight. I'd rather have them not talk at all except in the counseling session if they cannot talk without fighting. I ask them to practice their new techniques, and if they have a problem, to wait until they bring it in to me so they don't create more destruction while we are doing the work of rebuilding. If you have a strong habit of fighting in your marriage, and you're not working with a counselor, use the "What to do" sections below to change your couple dynamic. The many guidelines and exercises in this book were designed to teach you how to avoid fighting, but if you still find yourself arguing and want to change that habit, learn to identify destructive fighting and know the techniques to counter it. This will help you work toward conquering the arguing habit.

Destructive Fighting Habits

- *Blaming and accusing:* Fights based on blaming and accusing each other erode the connections between you. "You never do anything around here." "You didn't put gas in the car again!" "You're always making a mess!" There is nothing to be gained from blaming; it's a childish habit left over from grammar school. Even when you make up and forgive each other, the fact that you were willing to be mean to each other will register and not be forgotten, and the angry words are also remembered.

    - *What to do:* If your partner begins blaming you, don't respond. Don't defend yourself; it gives credibility to the accusations. Just sit passively or take a "time-out" per the instructions in chapter 5. If you're the one who's blaming, ask for what you want instead: "Please help me carry the groceries."

        "When you take the car, please put gas in it, or at least let me know if it's on empty."

        "After you are done with a dish, please put it in the dishwasher."

- *Nasty comments:* Zingers like "You'd forget your head if it wasn't screwed on!" "You're gaining weight, and it turns me off!" or "You're just like your (abusive) father!" are verbal violence and childish attempts to get the upper hand in the argument. They are also hurtful and can be remembered a long time by your spouse. If you're indulging in nastiness, don't expect to get any sex or affection from your partner—it's a tradeoff.

    - *What to do:* The best response is silence. Wait calmly until the attacker's energy is expended. Any response you make at this point will only fuel the attack. If it gets too out of hand, use the instructions for calling "time-out" as in chapter 5. If you're the one zinging, apologize sincerely as soon as you realize you're being nasty. Better yet, learn to catch yourself thinking those things before you say them. Even if you got away with saying such things to your siblings when you were young, you won't get away with it here. Find a more sensible expression of your anger: "I'm very frustrated right now, so I'm going to take a brisk walk. We'll talk later, when I can be more civil." Later, come back and use the Guidelines for Problem Solving in chapter 2 (page 41).

- *Sidetracking:* This is the technique you use when you don't want to take responsibility for a problem, and it's a common response to blaming. It's a way to divert the discussion from the real issue, "OK, so I didn't get home for dinner when I promised. But you were late last Sunday!" If you take this bait and start arguing about who's late more often, you'll both get more angry and the problem will never be solved. The issue of lateness will come up again and again for years, but handling it correctly will eliminate any unnecessary yelling.

  - *What to do:* Stay focused on the issue.

    You: "Let's not argue about who does it more, let's see what we can do to solve it. What if we each gave the other person fifteen minutes' grace, and then went on without them? So if you're late for dinner, and don't call, I'll give you fifteen minutes, then the kids and I will eat, and you'll have to have leftovers when you come home. If I'm late when we're going to go to the movies, you'll wait fifteen minutes, then go without me, and I'll have to drive myself there and find you."

    Your partner: "That sounds pretty good, but I still think it would be better to call if you're going to be late."

You: "I agree. We'll both make a better effort to call, but if that doesn't happen, this will be our backup."

- *Negative mind reading:* This is making up negative motives or thoughts for your partner and then accusing him or her. "I don't think where we go on vacation is the issue here. You just don't want me to have fun." Or "You didn't really want to help Natalie move her garbage cans. You were just avoiding talking to me." This is subtly nasty but couched in guilt-producing self-pity. It's not only very unattractive, but also very damaging to the trust between you.

  - *What to do:* If your partner reads your mind, don't take the bait and fight about it—instead, rise above it with a light response: "Nice mind reading, Dr. Freud, would you like to know what I really think?" Hopefully, your partner will look sheepish or smile, and you can then discuss the problem using the Guidelines for Reassurance in chapter 5 (page 122).

- *Contradiction of feelings:* This is a combination of mind reading and sidetracking, and tends to happen when you're sharing your feelings in a way that feels blaming to your partner: "I'm depressed because you ignore me." The contradictory response, "You're not really upset with me because I ignore you; you're upset because Susie wants me to help her do her homework, and not you." It's an attempt to avoid blame and to sidetrack the discussion at the same time. It leads to counterblaming and layer upon layer of accusations.

  - *What to do:* Don't be sucked into the never-ending battle over whose feelings are right. Instead, pause a moment to regroup, and use chapter 3's "I messages" and say, "These are my feelings, I'm sorry I blamed you for them, but I am concerned about a problem, and I want your help to solve it. Will you help?" Then use the Guidelines for Being Better Understood (chapter

4, page 90) to restate what is upsetting you and begin solving the problem.

And, worst of all:

• *Counterblaming:* Once one of you has accused or blamed the other, a common response is to accuse back.

> **You:** "You hurt my feelings."
>
> **Your partner:** "You're too sensitive, everything hurts your feelings."

This is an attempt to avoid being blamed by accusing the blamer of a worse sin. I hope it's obvious that this will go nowhere but down. It's the marital road to perdition. Tactics like this lead to all-out marriage wars that don't end until divorce.

- ■ *What to do:* Avoid a blaming response, no matter what it takes. If you have to call "time-out" and leave the room, do it. This argument must stop, NOW! After your cooling-off period, come back and use the Guidelines for Reassurance, Rewinding the Tape, and How to Let Go of Small Things (all from chapter 5, pages 122, 129, and 130), and Guidelines for Problem Solving in chapter 2 (page 41).

• *Power struggles:* All the power struggle tactics described in detail in chapter 5 (pages 120–21), guilt and obligation, threats and emotional blackmail, courtroom logic, peacekeeping, sacrificing, and hammering away, are also destructive fighting tactics.

- ■ *What to do:* Reread the section in chapter 5 to refresh and strengthen your awareness and learning.

Fair Fights

Thirty years of marriage counseling and twenty-five years of a second marriage have convinced me that fights are not necessary in a marriage. Married couples need to have discussions, they need to solve problems, and sometimes they need to disagree, but they don't need to argue, bicker, or fight. Fights are dramatic, which is not helpful to a discussion. If you have enough energy to create drama, you have more than enough to tone it down into a discussion. However, because social expectations and mythology are so strong, many of my clients want guidelines for "fighting fair." I've developed a set of Fair Fight Guidelines you may find helpful.

If you feel a fight is unavoidable, you can still find a win-win resolution if you follow these guidelines.

Fair Fight Guidelines

- Remember, the point of the fight is to reach a solution, not to win, be right, or make your partner wrong.
- Don't try to mind read. Instead ask what he or she is thinking.
- Don't bring up all the prior problems that relate to this one. Leave the past in the past; keep this about one recent problem. Solve one thing at a time.
- Keep the process simple. State the problem, suggest some alternatives, and choose a solution together.
- Don't talk too much at once. Keep your statements to two or three sentences. Your partner will not be able to grasp more than that.
- Give your partner a chance to respond and to suggest options.
- Practice equality. If something is important enough to one of you, it will inevitably be important to both of you. Honor your partner's need to solve a problem.
- Ask and answer questions directly. Again, keep it as simple as possible. Let your partner know you hear him or her.

- State your problem as a request, not a demand. To make it a positive request, use "I messages" and "please."
- Don't use power struggle tactics: guilt, obligation, threats, emotional blackmail, courtroom logic, and hammering away are off limits.
- Know your facts: If you're going to fight for something, know the facts about the problem. Do research, find out what options are available, and know how you feel and what would solve the problem for you.
- Ask for changes in behavior, don't criticize character, ethics, or morals.
- Don't fight over who's right or wrong. Opinions are opinions, and that won't solve the problem. Instead, focus on what will work.
- Ask your partner if he or she has anything to add to the discussion. "Is there anything else we need to discuss now?"
- Don't guess what your partner is thinking or feeling. Instead, ask, "What do you think?" Or "How do you feel about it?"
- Hold hands and look at each other. Remember, you're partners.
- If you're angry, express it calmly. "I'm angry about...." There's no need for drama, and it won't get you what you want. Anger is satisfied by being acknowledged and creating change. Anger is a normal emotion. Rage is phony. It's drama created by not taking care of yourself.
- Acknowledge and honor your partner's feelings—don't deflect them, laugh at them, or freak out. They're only feelings, and they subside when respected, heard, and honored.
- Listen with your whole self. Paraphrase what your partner says; check to see if you understand by repeating what is said. "So you are angry because you think I ignored you. Is that right?"

- No personal attacks or criticism. Focus on solving the problem.
- If you want to let off steam, ask permission to vent or take a time out. Handle your excess emotion or energy by being active (run, walk, hit a pillow), writing, or talking to someone who is not part of the problem. Don't direct it personally at anyone. You can't vent and solve problems at the same time.
- Don't try to solve a problem if you're impaired: tired, hungry, drunk, or unstable.
- Surrender to your responsibility. When you become aware that you have made a mistake, admit it and apologize. It is an opportunity to learn and grow.

Learning and Growing from Your Disagreements

Sometimes the people we love most are the most difficult for us to get along with. They're not bad people, others get along with them fine, and so do you—most of the time. But sometimes you have to work a little harder to understand what they mean and to not take what they say the wrong way. When your heart is at stake, it's scary when their personalities or styles are differ from yours. However, having differences with your partner or children will stretch you a bit and enrich your life and understanding in ways that the easy times don't. Challenging times in relationships can be the most rewarding when you understand they have a purpose.

Difficult People

Perhaps you have run into people who test your patience—co-workers, friends, or family. Sometimes people are difficult to handle because they remind you of other people you had problems with in the past, so you're attracted and frustrated at the same time. Others can be difficult for many people around them. Problems with a familiar type of person (that is, someone who has similar personality traits as your mother, sister, dad, or brother) may not emerge until you're already bonded and involved as friends or partners.

You can gain valuable insights and skills through overcoming negative reactions and learning to view someone as a reflection of yourself—a useful mirror. The following exercise will help you step back and look at others as a source of information about yourself, view people from a different angle, and use the very person who upset you as a reflection of the internal dynamics behind your struggles.

EXERCISE: Mirrors and Teachers

1. List people who can be difficult for you: Make a list of people with whom you have had problems in the recent past, or family members who are still presenting problems.

2. Choose a mirror: Select one of the most difficult people on the list, and think about your interaction with that person. What do you want from him or her? Do you want to be understood? To be respected? To be left alone? To be appreciated? To be cared about?

3. Relate it to yourself: Now consider how to give to yourself what you want from your "mirror." If you want to be left alone, do you leave yourself alone? That is, do you give yourself alone time and also refrain from badgering yourself? If you want to be trusted, do you trust yourself? If you want to be heard, do you listen to your own self? If you want to be important, are you important to you?

4. Change your self-treatment: Practice treating yourself the way you would want to be treated by your "mirror." For example, if you are angry because your spouse doesn't treat you with respect, consider what it would mean to treat yourself with respect. Change your behavior toward yourself accordingly. If you're upset because your spouse doesn't listen to you, spend some time every day listening to yourself.

5. Learn new skills: Think about the dynamics between your mirror and yourself, and what you need to learn that would improve the relationship. Perhaps you need to learn not to take what is said too seriously. Perhaps you need to learn to set boundaries or to handle someone's anger more effectively. Make a list of new skills you could learn that would improve your ability to deal better with your mirror, and go through the exercises and guidelines in this book to find what you need. Also note other places you could learn the skills you need. From a friend? With a therapist? From other books? Perhaps you could even take a class.

6. Do your part: Take responsibility for your part of the relationship. Keep in mind that no one can struggle with you if you don't struggle back. Consider what you need to do to remove yourself from the relationship problem. Remember, no matter what's going on, you have control over your own actions—you can choose not to participate in any situation that is destructive or counterproductive. Gaining the skill to handle people who are difficult for you will improve all your relationships. You can also use the Adult Time-Out technique in chapter 5 if the relationship gets too difficult for you. Learn to treat him or her as a member of someone else's family—with whom you would just politely ignore any obnoxious behavior.

Domestic Violence

Domestic violence happens in far too many marriages. Violence occurs in marriages of all economic levels, ethnic groups, and levels of education and status. If the destructive tactics above are an everyday occurrence in your marriage, or if they escalate into raging and violence, you must act to stop the problem right away. The following steps will help you.

What to Do If You or Your Children Are Battered

1. Realize it's not going to get better. If your partner flies into a rage, verbally or sexually abuses you or your children—no matter what he or she may say—it isn't your fault. You have no control over his or her behavior. Even the abuser has very little control. It is not just a one-time incident, it is an indication of a severely disturbed character, and it will not go away without intense therapy.

2. Protect yourself and your children. The best way to do this is to tell the truth to family, friends, your minister, your doctor, your therapist, your co-workers, one of the hotlines listed below, the police, and anyone else who will listen. There is no need for you to be ashamed, but there is an urgent need for you to get help. If it seems that no one is listening, consider that you might not be telling the whole truth—battered spouses have a tendency to downplay and make excuses for the abuser. The best protection for you and your children is for your abuser's behavior to become public knowledge. The vast majority of abusers are cowards who only prey on dependent, defenseless people. They like to believe they are in control, and they aren't as likely to lose control before witnesses.

3. Once you have been physically abused, do not be alone with the abuser again. This is another reason to tell everyone you know. You either need a place to go or someone (perhaps several people) to stay with you until you are safe. You may also need financial help. There are shelters you can go to that will keep you safe. Look in the front of your phone book or ask the operator for a domestic violence hotline and call to find a shelter.

4. **If you are hit, call the police.** The law is now on your side. When they arrive, press charges. Do not make excuses to yourself or anyone else. If your abuser gets away with it even once, he or she will get more abusive. Do not listen to pleas for sympathy, understanding, or forgiveness. You can forgive the abuser after he or she has gotten help, and only after you and your children are safe.

5. **If you or a child are injured, get medical help.** Tell the doctors and nurses the truth about how it happened.

6. **File a restraining order or a Protection from Violence Order.** Volunteers at the police department will help you fill out the forms. With a restraining order, you can call the police as soon as the abuser gets close to you or your home. Without one, the police need evidence of the abuse to arrest anyone.

7. **Attend Al-Anon meetings.** You will learn a lot of good information that will help you avoid being someone else's victim. For information, go to: *www.al-anon.org*. Or ask the operator for the domestic violence hotline and you will be referred to a local chapter.

Choosing Your Own Responses

All of this requires learning to choose your own actions and behave according to your own high standards in your life, your marriage, and other relationships, no matter what the other people are doing.

Each of us has his or her own sphere of influence, our own private space, which we can picture as a physical boundary surrounding us, like the invisible "glass wall" mimes often pretend to be trapped behind. All other people and events are outside this boundary but visible and accessible through it. You can send messages in the form of words and deeds (and perhaps even thoughts and subtle body and facial movements) through this boundary, and others can send messages in to you. You have little control over what people choose to send toward you but total control over what you choose to send out. The control you do have over what people send into your world consists in how you receive it and respond to it. There are two ways you can control how others respond to you: (1) You can ask them for what you want, understanding you may get "no" for an answer, or (2) you can act in ways that get you the responses you want.

For example, if your spouse or your boss is cranky with you, you can't change the fact that some crabbiness has been sent your way. Perhaps there is some other problem (having nothing to do with you) that accounts for this bad mood. There is little to be gained from attempting to mind read or to change the other person's attitude.

However, if you remember about your own private space, and your wall, you will realize you have many options.

- You can choose to believe that the other person meant to hurt you.
- You can believe he or she is your enemy.
- You can feel you somehow deserve to be treated that way.

Any of the above choices will lead to a negative, hurtful response from you and most likely to an unpleasant interaction. Or you can choose not to worry about the reason for the crabbiness, and instead assume it is a problem the other person is having and become helpful. "Are you upset?" "Is there anything I can do to help?" "Will you explain to me what you're upset about?" If you choose to respond this way, you are more likely to have a good, productive talk with the other person.

Self-Control

Making these choices requires exercising your power of self-control. Controlling your own reactions and responses is not always easy to manage. In the face of your partner's actions, it's difficult not to react. Learning to stop and think, to respond thoughtfully and carefully rather than quickly and automatically, requires some thought and practice (the Reframing Exercise, in chapter 1, page 10 is great for this) and may seem hard at first. But learning self-control, no matter how difficult, is always worthwhile because it makes every moment of your life easier.

Self-control begins with self-awareness. If you already know what pushes your buttons, you will be less reactive to it. If you can tell when you're stressed, you can be more cautious at those times. If you know that you and your partner tend to fight about the same things, over and over, you can learn to exercise more self-control when those things are discussed and react differently to avoid fighting.

It is not necessary to keep tight self-control all the time. If you and your partner are relaxing and having fun, you can most likely respond spontaneously and be fine. But, if you're in a tense situation, extra tired, frustrated, stressed, or talking about a sensitive subject, thinking about your response in advance will make the whole interaction work a lot better.

For example, if the two of you are just relaxing in the hot tub, hiking in the woods, at a ball game, or relaxing under a tree, you can probably feel free to tease your partner, joke around, and be playful. But if you're talking about financial problems or jealousy, your responses need to be much more carefully considered.

As long as you remember that your responses will go a long way toward shaping the whole interaction, and eventually your whole relationship, and you take the time to control the way you respond, you will see all your relationships improve dramatically. This kind of self-control is a very powerful tool when used correctly. By using it wisely, you gain the power to make your relationships, and therefore your life, happier, more successful, and more loving.

When you've spent a lifetime fighting and struggling or been influenced by generations of couples (such as parents and grandparents) who believed fighting was their only option, it may seem very strange to think you can just stop struggling with each other, but if you consistently use the techniques you have learned in this chapter, you really can end the habit of fighting and squabbling. Imagine how pleasant it would be to face any discussion with confidence that it will not become a power struggle, fight, or screaming match. Instead, you and your partner can simply discuss the pros and cons, your different ideas, perceptions, and opinions and reach a logical and mutually agreed-upon solution to any problem you face. For this reason, it's worth confronting and changing any family patterns you have learned, or habits you've developed together. The next chapter will help you do just that.

Chapter 7

THE ROOT CAUSES
OF STRUGGLING

Like most of my clients, you probably entered your relationship madly in love, convinced that your feelings for each other were so strong they would carry you through into a marriage that included mutual responsibility, mutual concern for each other, successful problem solving, partnership, teamwork, easy communication, support, satisfaction, and fidelity.

But most relationships fail to live up to these dreams because people run into problems that they do not know how to handle, like Daisy and Mike.

Daisy and Mike were sweethearts in college and married young, with the support of both families and a big celebration with all their friends. They had a "dream relationship" and high hopes for happiness. Now thirty-five and a working wife, Daisy has spent most of her adult life taking care of others, especially Mike, but feels unworthy of receiving attention and doesn't realize that it is equally important to take care of herself. Meanwhile Mike, a thirty-eight-year-old factory worker, has trouble showing affection, and since he isn't demonstrative and supportive toward Daisy, she feels depleted and unresponsive toward him. It doesn't take long for them both to feel deprived and neglected, and their relationship becomes an unbearable situation. Because they haven't been able to sustain their good feelings toward each other, they both feel disappointed and guilty.

The desperation Daisy and Mike feel is not unusual, and fighting can make any relationship feel more like a nightmare than a dream, especially when you and your partner struggle with different wants and needs. If you don't know how to work together effectively to solve the conflict, the resulting frustration, anger, and arguments can make your marriage more and more unpleasant and difficult to sustain.

Developmental Stages of Relationships

Mythology in our culture and in popular media presents love and relating in a "happily ever after" way. In the love story, a couple meets, perhaps they have problems and misunderstandings, but soon they realize they're in love, and they live "happily ever after." No one really talks or thinks about what happens next. But in real life, relationships develop in stages, even after marriage. The love stories focus only on the early stages: meeting, dating, courtship, and commitment, marriage, and the honeymoon phase, where everything is brand new and wonderful. This is what romantic songs and movies are all about, and it has become what people call "being in love." Extending the honeymoon phase indefinitely is what people fantasize as "happily ever after."

Couples who have not had lasting relationships before have no experience and few models of the later phases of developing intimacy, and settled partnership.

Development of Intimacy

As your relationship continues and deeper intimacy develops past the first two years, your love will mature and become less of a romantic fantasy about hopes and dreams and more reality based, about what you know you can achieve with your partner. This is the stage where the sexual rush subsides, the magic fades, and both of you begin to relax and show your innermost, less perfect selves. You're beginning to get to know the deeper, more reality-based aspects of each other, warts and all. After the rush of new relationship excitement and one new milestone after another, things begin to slow down, and you may be surprised to feel vulnerable and awkward with each other. In this stage, you may argue, struggle for power, and become irritable and unreasonable. The fear arises that you will not be able to sustain the romantic picture you've drawn for each other, and that your mate will not like this more realistic view of you. As a result, both partners need (and each has trouble providing) reassurance and personal space. Many relationships struggle in this stage, and some don't survive, because if the partners don't understand or expect this change, it can feel like something has gone wrong developmentally and your love has failed to blossom into the dream you hoped for.

If you don't have the tools to solve the problems that arise, you can become discouraged and hopeless. Couples who hang in there and work through their problems with mutual concern and caring find that they've reached a new level of intimacy and security they never felt before. In fact, research is now showing that couples who don't get discouraged and who hang in there with each other, can overcome problems, develop teamwork, and learn to enjoy each other more.

The previous chapters in this book have given you tools and guidelines to help you work through the problems of developing true intimacy and begin to develop your own, unique working process and ways of being close and getting things done. As you achieve those goals and develop a real partnership with each other, you'll feel more secure and more settled.

Settled Partnership

Then the issues of the settled partnership arise: As you relax into deep familiarity and intimacy, you'll begin to wonder how to keep love alive over a long period of time, how not to take each other for granted, how to set goals beyond just being together, and how to handle changes.

Settled partnership is the stage where the enormous pleasures of lasting love are realized. When you reach this point successfully, you and your partner will know you're loved as you really are, with all your minor faults and issues. You will be experts in living life together. When you have learned to work together as partners, focusing on what works, not blaming or finding fault, and aiming for mutual satisfaction, you'll have a feeling of security, intimacy, and partnership that's truly satisfying and rewarding. When problems arise, you'll have the wisdom and experience to keep your commitment alive through teamwork and mutual understanding.

Usually, it takes several years to achieve the full benefits of these later stages. Unless you've been through a long-term relationship before, the difficulties encountered in the development of the intimacy stage and the settled partnership phase will come as a surprise, so it's easy to be discouraged and give up. People who learn and grow from their experiences often do much better in their second or third long-term relationship, because their early experience taught them what to expect and gave them a chance to acquire the necessary long-term skills. Because we lack education and experience, our early unsuccessful relationships often serve as practice for later successful ones.

The good news is that now there is a "technology" of relationships, a series of skills and attitudes that have been researched and found effective. The study of the psychology of relationships is a relatively new science, and as with most new fields of study, it was the problems (areas of relationships that created pain and trouble) that both researchers and clinical psychologists focused on. Not until psychologists found ways of alleviating the pain and eliminating destructive behaviors, and began to find some solutions, did we begin to focus on developing healthy models. Now that healthy models have been identified and specific techniques and tools have proven effective, it's quite simple for you to learn what causes struggling and what will fix it. Learning proven relationship skills can help the later relationship stages develop more smoothly and faster.

Let's look first at the root causes of struggling.

Lack of Skills

Relationships often develop trouble because couples who get together have rarely had a chance to learn the necessary skills for healthy relationships, creating families, and raising children. Such personal issues are not usually discussed in school, and at home parents often conceal their intimate interactions and relationship issues from their children, so we grow up with only a vague idea of what it takes to create a healthy relationship. Even relationship counselors tend to focus on resolving each individual's problems rather than on teaching couple skills. So most couples learn about relationships by the example of those around them, who often fight, split up, or are clearly dishonest with each other. Or they acquire their relationship models through media images—either unrealistically happy and harmonious couples, or dramatic dysfunction: infidelity, addiction, fighting, and passion. Such models provide little useful information about how to form a healthy working partnership between equals.

It's easy to look around and see many relationships—our parents, our friends, in movies, and on TV—that seem to be full of struggle, pain, boredom, and fraught with problems.

Struggling relationships often look scary and lopsided when any of the following situations take hold.

- One partner gives and the other takes.
- One is an addict, alcoholic, or gambler and the other pays the price.
- One partner overpowers, coerces, defrauds, deceives, or takes advantage of the other.
- Both partners follow rigid roles that seem to alter or stifle their personalities.
- One gives up a career to support a spouse, who succeeds and then leaves.
- Both partners seem filled with anger, contempt, hostility, or hatred of the other.
- Both compromise their needs for the survival of the marriage.
- Both withhold their true thoughts and feelings because "it would hurt my partner," and they then feel dissatisfied.
- One or both are numb, depressed, or detached, and they are partners only in that they stay together "for the children" or because they feel they "have to."
- The romance is gone and there is no vitality.
- Their sexual needs and differences seem to conflict, creating emotional suffering for both.
- One or both have affairs to fill a missing ingredient in their partnership.

These difficult relationships get our attention because they're dramatic, and often the drama is played out in public. All the above scenarios happen because the couple is too emotionally immature or they just don't have the skills to work through their difficulties, so they fumble through their problems unsuccessfully, creating and repeating dysfunctional patterns.

Learning to Cooperate Rather Than Compete

Most of the trouble between intimate partners happens because they don't know how to work together to solve problems. When one or both of you try to be "in charge" and have more than half the power, discussions become power struggles. You can tell you're in a power struggle when you fight bitterly over disagreements because you're struggling to be in control, or else you avoid discussing problems altogether because it isn't worth the struggle. Power struggles mean you and your partner spend a lot of time either fighting for what you want or feeling deprived. You may also have witnessed your parents, friends, or neighbors interacting in this way, because it's a common mistake couples make.

The frustration, resentment, anger, disappointment, and despair in competitive, struggling relationships almost always stem from not being able to get what you want from your relationship and from each other. While this feels unfair and inappropriate, in real life it happens frequently. A couple unskilled in working together to solve problems could easily become tangled in a web of blaming, hurt, and anger and, after years of similar unresolved conflicts, can build a backlog of bitterness that can't be healed.

Repetitive, unresolved fights about money, sex, affection, time, jealousy, family, coming out, raising children, housekeeping, or other problems, and not being able to reach a mutually agreeable or satisfying solution will keep you locked in habitual ways of relating that create dissatisfaction and struggle between you.

In a competitive relationship, you and your partner believe you have to fight for what you want and that you can't work together to create intimacy, respect, and mutual satisfaction. Because this competitive attitude is so ingrained in each of us, it usually takes a shift in belief and a lot of practice to learn how to stop fighting, arguing, and insisting you are right or to stop being afraid you won't get what you want.

Couples compete because both parties believe that someone has to "win" in a discussion. Some children learn that they must be the best and try hard or manipulate to get what they want, which causes them to either struggle to win or to give up. We become used to competing for jobs, dates, and in sports; we even compete with ourselves to see if we can outdo our previous efforts. When competition is stimulating, motivating, and fun, it is healthy.

Between partners in intimate relationships, however, competition becomes stressful, counterproductive, and toxic, poisoning the relationship by turning you and your partner into adversaries and undermining the mutual support and encouragement vital to creating a partnership. Expectations that are too high (trying to maintain two careers, a spectacularly exciting sex life, and eternal youth, while also raising children) also create pressure that leads to competition.

To create a truly loving partnership you must learn several skills:

- You must develop good communication skills, including understanding the difference between problem solving and fighting.
- You need to understand that marriage takes work and emotional maturity. That means you have to handle yourself at least as well as you do at work, and maybe even better.
- You need to learn how to calm down when you become too emotional so that you can have a sensible discussion rather than a fight.
- You have to know how to reach a mutually satisfactory agreement. That means you need to understand what

your partner wants as well as what you want and to work together to make sure both of you are satisfied.

- You must be able to keep your agreements or renegotiate them if you find they don't work. This builds trust and security in your partnership.
- You need to know how to comfort and reassure each other in times of stress rather than bicker because you're worried.
- You must choose to create a loving atmosphere rather than a competitive edginess between you—to bring more sweetness and less strife into your home.
- And you need to know when and where to get help to solve problems that are beyond your ability as partners.

In the earlier chapters of this book, you learned the relationships skills that are most needed, just as the couples who are my clients do in the counseling office. Couples come to me daily with what they believe are unsolvable problems, and almost always a solution can be found. Because I know how to help each couple explore all the underlying wants, break free from old, problem-creating behaviors, and eliminate the false limitations they have placed on the problem, the solution arises easily out of the sharing of information and wants and the dynamics of the situation.

If you follow the guidelines and use the steps of the exercises in the previous chapters, you can learn the skills you may not have known until now.

If you use the guidelines and exercises until you are comfortable and capable with them, you'll be able to solve problems together successfully and work together as a team rather than struggle against each other. Making sure you have family and financial meetings will help keep you on track and prevent both of you from sliding back into old habits. As you develop more partnership and cooperation and learn from each other through the years, you'll create a functional, settled, partnership that will support and sustain both of you through the daily ups and downs of life.

If you look carefully enough, you can find many couples who do know how to create loving, workable relationships, and together, you and they can create a mutually helpful and supportive team to strengthen each other's good relationship habits and share what you learn and new effective tools. You can learn to work out mutually satisfactory solutions to whatever problems you're facing by working together to ensure each other's satisfaction and making room in your relationship for individual differences, preferences, and tastes.

Couples who know how to solve problems effectively and cooperatively together have significantly fewer fights, are more satisfied in their relationship, and feel more understood and cared about by their partners. Knowing you and your partner can solve problems together means having the confidence that the two of you can face life's ups and downs better together than either of you could alone. The old adage "two heads are better than one," which is often not true, becomes the truth in marriage when your two heads and hearts become a great team.

Working together productively promotes an atmosphere of congeniality, friendship, and teamwork. Couples who don't spend time struggling, fighting, or creating power plays have more time and energy to have fun, laugh, have playful sex, and generally get a lot more done. Couples who can problem solve together also help each other to think clearly and avoid mindlessness.

When you and your partner cooperate, you'll create a marriage in which each of you gets what you want and both of you feel cared about and considered. That is exactly the emotional climate you need to create a lasting relationship, because who would leave a partner who is so much fun and who will work together to solve any problems that arise? Instead of being a struggle or something to avoid, solving such problems will become an opportunity to reaffirm your mutual love and caring, and to strengthen your partnership and teamwork.

You can have a successful partnership even when one or both of you still have some personal emotional problems that are unresolved. Working together, you can help each other overcome individual problems (whether they are emotional, from past history, work-related, or stem from some other part of your separate lives), and you can make enough room in your relationship that your moods and personalities can coexist without undue struggle. As you develop more mutuality and cooperation, your sense of inner equality will grow and further enhance your relationship, in an ever-increasing spiral.

Even if you encounter a problem that is too severe or long-standing to be solved by mutual discussion between the two of you, you can seek help, and a professional with an objective viewpoint can help you get on the right track.

The key to achieving this enhanced level of partnership, and to keep it growing, is to focus on learning from your interactions with each other. The following metaphor will help you see your relationship and its problems and successes as an opportunity to learn.

How to Learn from Love

Everyone has a lot to learn from love. Understanding and accepting that your intimate relationship will stretch you and cause you to grow will help you create more intimacy and a better sense of partnership.

Of all the learning opportunities in life, intimate, lifelong relationships can perhaps teach us the most. Approaching your relationship as if you're a student of love and not expected to be an expert, and viewing problems as exercises for learning, you'll find solving problems is much easier, your personal growth is faster, and intimacy makes more sense.

To approach your marriage as a course in personal growth, begin by re-evaluating why you're together. Use it as a training ground and view your partner as a teacher who showed up in your life to help you learn something. Assume there will be a lot to learn and lots of problems to solve that increase in complexity as you gain in knowledge. Never do the problems indicate that either of you deserve punishment, have done something bad. They only show that you have something to learn, and they even give you the means to learn it. Every single problem will have a valuable lesson within it if you are willing to learn from it. You might learn something about yourself; you might gain emotional maturity, patience, or the inner strength you need to stand up for yourself calmly.

As in any learning situation, if you do not understand the lesson and solve the problem, you will keep getting it back in altered forms until you do understand. This is *not* to give you a hard time, but to teach you what you need to know to live a fuller, more loving life.

Doing Your Homework

When problems arise, stop a moment and think before you react with outrage and hurt. Say to yourself, "What was I given this problem for? What can I learn from this? What do I need to know to solve it?" View the problem as a homework assignment and figure out what it has been designed to teach you.

For example, perhaps your spouse is not giving you enough attention. Perhaps this situation has happened before, with this partner and within other relationships. You merely want a kind word, a loving touch; it doesn't seem too much to ask. Yet this partner, and perhaps friends and family members, too, seem to find it impossible. What could you possibly learn from this problem?

Perhaps the problem of not enough attention means you need to learn more about networking, having a circle of friends you can rely on so that your primary relationship is not under the strain and stress of having to meet *all* your needs. When your partner is preoccupied with work problems, illness, or other absorbing facets of life, you can still have many sources of affection and attention.

Learning to Love Yourself

Often lack of attention means you need to learn the great satisfaction of being able to give attention to *yourself*. When you are unable to care about yourself satisfactorily, the resulting neediness causes other people to feel a sense of despair about loving you. A lack of self-love makes a person feel like a bottomless pit into which others can pour all their love and not be able to fill it. Frustrated, they give up trying. Learning the lesson of self-love eliminates the problem. It is easy to be successful in loving a person who knows self-love, and everyone loves to be successful.

A deficit of attention might mean you need to learn the art of appreciation, noticing the attention you are given, however slight it may seem. That which is appreciated grows and grows. Again, people quickly tire of giving that which goes unnoticed. A little appreciation of what is right is a lot more attractive and effective than complaining about what is wrong. Many of the exercises in this book are about learning what you can from your relationships with others.

There are many other examples of the knowledge to be gained from solving this one attention issue. The more carefully and conscientiously you approach your homework, the more you will benefit in increased love and joy.

The Basic Lesson

The most important step you can take toward making your relationship a course in personal growth is to decide that your partner and every other person close to you is a friend who is assisting you in your major task of learning. Each of these friends has lessons of their own to learn with your help. You can regard your spouse and all your friends and family as a mutual helping-learning-growing group. Problems and struggles then become mutual learning opportunities.

Try saying, in the middle of a problem, "I don't know what this is all about, but I know I love you, and we both have something to learn from this, and I'd like to find out what it is," and you'll see the anxiety and stress drain out of the situation.

Healing Wounds

Healing hurt feelings is another art that you can learn from your marriage. Human beings are imperfect and clumsy; we often stumble and hurt each other. The closer we get, the more likely we are to bruise each other emotionally. It's almost guaranteed that your feelings will be hurt repeatedly in an intimate relationship, even though your partner loves you. With practice, you can learn to heal yourself individually, and you and your partner can work together to heal each other. One example in this book is the Guidelines for Healing from Infidelity in chapter 3, on page 77. Whenever you are hurt or upset in a relationship situation, think about it before you react. Were you really hurt because your partner ignored you at the party, or is it really because communication has not been good for the past week and the party was an easy target for your blame? Find out if your hurt comes from where you first thought or if it's possibly an old hurt from another relationship or from childhood. Once you understand your hurt feelings, share them gently with your partner—no accusations—just a statement of your experience.

If you get agreement, then quite often a simple talk can point out the differences between then and now. Sometimes sharing your clarity becomes the healing. After sharing and talking, seek to figure out a way that you can be protected next time. You'll find that as soon as you know how to protect yourself, all the hurt and anger fade quickly.

A Good Teacher Can Help

Most education processes require a teacher, or at least a mentor. Intimacy is a fine art for which we are largely untrained, and many of the role models and guidelines in our society are highly toxic and negative. If you feel stuck in your life or your relationships, don't hesitate to find a teacher, a therapist, or other source of information to use as a guide. Books, classes, and workshops can also be very helpful. In addition, there are many wonderful guides and counselors around to help you. Get help in solving problems before they become too large. You deserve to have help with anything that feels difficult or unsolvable. Mastery of any art, including intimacy, usually benefits from a good teacher.

When you sign up for your course in personal growth, it's a lifetime study. Have fun with it. Love and joy are the goals; you can reach them if you do your work well, and graduate *magna cum laude*.

Chapter 8

MATURING IN LOVE

In the previous chapters, we discussed the main reasons couples fight and some effective solutions for those specific problems, plus a discussion of the root causes of most difficulties. But in the course of a long relationship, many divisive issues can arise that may not have been covered. In this chapter, you'll learn some information, techniques, and guidelines to help you understand why you might be having difficulty and to teach you how to resolve problems about almost anything. It's like graduate study for your course in creating a successful marriage.

The Mature Relationship

If you and your partner are fighting over little things that don't make sense, if one of you suddenly "blows up" or gets angry and the other one doesn't understand why, if either of you is prone to throwing tantrums or pouting or getting even, if you're unwilling to take responsibility for your actions or unwilling to discuss problems, or if you feel very unsatisfied and restless in your relationship, consider that one or both of you may have some confusion about the difference between a childlike definition of love and a more mature definition of love between equal, adult partners.

We all learned about love and family before we were old enough to think clearly. Consequently, our reactions in emotional familial relationships and marriage tend to be childlike. We react without thinking, often in defensive, blaming, and irrational ways. Most of us are different in situations such as work, where we think before we speak. This is because we were much older when we learned about work and had more ability to control ourselves and choose our reactions. Your marriage will benefit greatly, and you'll have an easier time, if you bring those work skills into your home and learn to respond more thoughtfully, rather than reacting emotionally when there's a problem. You learned the basics of how to do this in chapter 2 in the Guidelines for Using Business Skills at Home.

To make your relationship more lasting and more satisfying, the following information about mutuality will help you examine your definition of love to determine how mature it is and how you can improve your interaction as partners.

Mutual Commitment

Mature love is based on mutual commitment, which has several components: mutual love, mutual trust, mutual benefit, and mutual support. Commitment is more than just promising to be faithful to each other. To be committed to your marriage means you both pledge to work together to make the marriage work for both of you. True commitment—to produce the motivation and devotion necessary to sustain a long, healthy relationship—is a state of being, which cannot be forced no matter how much you or your partner would like it to be.

Commitment is not something you can demand from each other, because it is based on feeling. If you don't personally feel committed to creating a working partnership with each other, you won't be able to live up to your responsibilities, and, therefore, you won't get much satisfaction out of your marriage. As with any other endeavor, you get results according to how much you put in. When you're determined to create a successful marriage, you'll care as much about your partner's satisfaction as you do about your own. We call this equal caring about each other mutuality. A commitment based on mutuality does not falter, does not unravel, and is relatively easy to maintain because keeping it feels natural, good, and appropriate. It is a commitment we feel proud to make and to keep. Mature love is mutually caring, mutually giving, and mutually responsible, without the dependent, needy, or controlling imbalance of power present in the immature model. When you take responsibility for making love mutually satisfying, and expect equal maturity, responsibility, and respect from your partner, you increase your power to receive and give love at full capacity, while retaining your self-esteem and sense of competence.

Responsibility = Response-ability

In emotional situations, like marriage, most people have a tendency to react rather than to respond. When you react emotionally, allowing your first impulse to be expressed, you'll probably act in a childlike manner. It is much more effective and much less stressful on yourself and your partner if you both learn to respond in a more mature fashion.

Being a grownup in your marriage means you are responsible for everything you say and do and you are in charge of yourself and your life. Love is one of the areas of life where many of us have trouble remembering to act as adults, take responsibility for ourselves, and honor our responsibility toward each other.

Responsibility can be an emotionally loaded word. Often, people react to it the same way they would to the word *fault* or *blame*, as though saying "you're responsible for your life" means "you should feel guilty about your life." This sense of responsibility is childlike, reacting and responding as though an angry parent were standing over you saying, "Who's responsible for this mess?"

Adult responsibility is something else altogether. It often helps to think of it as response-ability, that is, the ability to respond to life. Seen this way, it's not blame; it acknowledges the fact that each person, in every circumstance, has an ability to think and choose his or her response. Response-ability is remembering to be in charge in an adult way, to make careful, thought-out choices, understanding that there are many possible responses and you can choose the one you make. When you respond in an adult manner to the events that occur in your relationship, not only will you make better decisions and have a more successful result, but also you and your spouse are more likely to develop healthy, effective patterns of interaction. For example, if your partner has a bad day and comes home cranky, you have choices: You can respond like a hurt or angry child, and most likely cause a fight, or you can respond like an adult and realize that your partner probably needs a few moments alone to recover from the day. After a short while, your spouse will calm down and the two of you can relax and enjoy the evening together. In this way, taking response-ability can enhance the time you spend together.

The Components of Mutuality

In relationships that work, true love is measured by mutual love, mutual trust, mutual benefit, and mutual support. In a mature relationship, you and your mate will be able to talk about what you want, and make agreements that both of you can keep.

Let's look at what those four mutualities are, and then explore how to develop or enhance them.

- *Mutual love:* Love is the constantly renewing energy that keeps your commitment alive. When both partners feel loved, and both feel appreciated for being loving, commitment can thrive. The key is to understand what giving and receiving love look like. I like the following two psychologists' definitions of love:

- "Love is the power within us that affirms and values another human being as he or she is," writes Robert Johnson in *We: Understanding the Psychology of Romantic Love* (1983).
- "Love . . . handles all things equally," writes Hugh Prather in *The Quiet Answer* (1982). "All of love must be given in order for all of it to remain. . . . There is only one kind of love, the uncalculated kind."

- *Mutual trust:* As your relationship progresses, both of you will have opportunities to demonstrate trustworthiness. If you both keep your promises and respect each other's wants and feelings, the trust between you grows. In order for love and commitment to exist, each partner in a marriage must trust the other.

- *Mutual benefit:* Obviously, not too many people will stay where they perceive no benefit to themselves. The benefit in your marriage may be emotional, financial, mental, or spiritual, and it's usually a combination of these. Each partner may perceive different benefits, but the benefits of the marriage must feel approximately equal to support commitment rather than resentment.

- *Mutual support:* Commitment implies stress. That is, when we feel committed, we feel willing to face the difficulties, the ups and downs of life, and the challenges of "working it out." Implicit in our commitment is the understanding that we will support each other to the best of our abilities, through good times and bad, and each of us will be responsible for ourselves and thus not lean too heavily on the other.

When all four kinds of mutuality are present in your inter-action and you feel them spontaneously, without pressure or coercion, you have the necessary conditions for true commit-ment. If you're really paying attention to whether you and your partner feel love, trust, benefit, and support, your intuition will probably be a pretty good indicator. Most of my clients report that they know when their relationship is unfair and unequal, even if they don't know what to do about it. Building fair-ness, partnership, and mutuality begins with wanting it. If you really desire to love each other as equals, and act accordingly, your mutual caring and appreciation will grow. Here are some guidelines for building mutuality.

Guidelines for Building Mutuality
To Build Mutual Love

Today's popular culture is cynical and "cool"—expressions of love are often looked on as embarrassing and awkward. But keeping love alive and flowing in your relationship is essential to being happy with each other. Set aside your reluctance and let each other know when you feel loved, and appreciate (with verbal thanks, with flowers and candy, with dinners out, with a hug or a kiss) your spouse's efforts to love you. Think in terms of ramping up the sweetness in your marriage. No matter how awkward you feel at first, you'll soon enjoy being in the loving atmosphere that results. If you're not getting the kind of love you want, use the problem-solving techniques in chapter 2 to discuss and solve the problem. We often need to teach each other how to love in the way we want to be loved. To explore this further, you can use the Giving and Receiving Love exer-cises that follow on pages 183 and 185.

If you're worried that your partner isn't feeling loved or appreciated, don't let it pass. Ask about it. Bring it up, whether you think you are getting a less than fair deal or a more than fair deal. You are setting your patterns here for the rest of your relationship. Once you start feeling that your relationship is unequal, if you don't talk about it, you'll begin to store up anger and resentment. Sooner or later, those stored-up feelings will explode and create a problem between you. Talking about it when the problem is small makes it much easier to solve. It may just be a simple misunderstanding. Don't let it become a battle.

The essence of mutuality is that you care about each other's satisfaction as much as about your own. To ask, describe what has you worried: "You've been a little distant this week, and I'm wondering if you know I love you, and if I'm showing you in the way you want." If you get reassured ("Oh, yes, I know you love me—I've been worrying about this presentation at work."), you'll know everything is OK. Or, if your partner says, "Yes, my feelings have been hurt because of what you said," you can work through the problem and heal the hurt, using the Steps to Forgiving exercise in chapter 3.

To Build Mutual Trust

To build trust, it's your actions, not your words, that count. You can make promises to be more reliable, but what will build trust is actually acting on the promises. Make sure you only make agreements you can actually keep. Renegotiate in advance if something prevents you from keeping your promises. Be willing to say "no" when you mean no. Help your partner to be honest by being willing to take "no" for an answer to your requests. Questions that can't take "no" for an answer are actually demands, or power plays. If you're going to make a demand, at least make an honest one. Saying "I demand that you take out the garbage now, and I'll be really angry if you don't" isn't nice, but it is more honest than saying, "Honey, would you please take the garbage out?" and then getting really angry if the garbage isn't taken out. While it's better to only make requests, at least honest demands don't damage mutual trust the way dishonest ones do.

To Build Mutual Benefit

Ask, "What's in it for me? And what's in it for you?" Consider whether decisions you are making will benefit both of you. For example, if one of you decides to work to put the other through school, what's the payoff for the wage earner? Does the student act the role of homemaker and do all the cooking and cleaning? Does the present wage earner get to be the student later? What agreement will even the benefits? Or if you ask your spouse to come visit your difficult family, what can you do in return? Using this kind of consideration on a daily basis ensures that both of you benefit equally most of the time.

Don't let unfairness go. Don't allow martyrdom or power plays into the relationship. No matter how tempted you are to coerce or demand your partner into doing it your way, resist the temptation. No matter how hard it is to stand up for your rights, learn to do it. Inequality now will cause relationship problems later.

To Build Mutual Support

Discuss what support means to each of you. Support can be emotional (such as a shoulder to cry on, or a hug), mental (help making a tough decision, talking it over), or physical (jogging together to lose weight, financial support). Find out which kinds mean the most to each of you and experiment with new ways to support each other. In chapter 10, you'll learn about the relationship reservoir, which is a useful metaphor for thinking about mutual support.

To reinforce the mutuality in your relationship, it's very valuable to understand how each of you gives and receives love. The following exercises will help you understand your own style of loving and also that of your partner.

Giving and Receiving Love

No matter what your past experience has been, making a relationship work is not as difficult as you may think. As I discussed earlier, most people have a tendency to love in reactive and responsive ways, that is, to just respond to whatever happens without thinking about what it means. In business, we don't just respond without thinking and let our emotional reactions rule our intellect, because we tend to think through our actions and decisions when they involve work or money. But in love, it's common to act on feelings without thinking. That doesn't work any better in your love life than it would in your career.

Here are some simple steps to follow that will increase your chances of success, no matter who you are, or whom you are seeking. You may want to set aside a notebook just for these exercises and record your progress.

EXERCISE 1: Receiving Love

Each of us has a different need for giving and receiving love. To create the kind of relationship you really want, you need to understand your personal definition of love. You and your spouse can each follow the steps and then use these exercises as a basis for discussion.

Think back over your life from childhood to today. Call up all the times you felt loved. (Even if you had a miserable childhood, there will be loving moments.) Every kindness shown by friends, teachers, grandparents, extended family, neighbors, or others counts. You can even use scenes from books, movies, and television to imagine words, actions, and events that symbolize love to you. Take the time to do this thoroughly. Fantasies and reminiscences become richer when you stay with them for a while. When you have a collection of scenes, words, and gestures that symbolize love to you, write them down in list form.

Your list might look something like this.

Love Is:

Being understood

Physical affection (hugs, a gentle touch)

Great sex

Time spent with someone special

Sentimental gifts

Eye-to-eye contact

A surprise party

Quiet talks

The whole family together at dinner

Phone calls for no special reason

A card game with silly jokes and laughter

Knowing when to leave me alone, and when to offer comfort

An energetic game of tag, hide-and-seek, or touch football

You can continue to add to this and let it grow. The more you know about what feels loving to you, the easier it will be to recognize when you see it and to negotiate and work it out with your partner. When you understand specifically what feels loving to you, you can teach each other how to love more effectively.

To understand your personal style of giving love, repeat the previous exercise to find out times and situations when you felt loving. Don't be surprised if this varies a bit from feeling loved. Giving and receiving are often different. Go through memories, movies, and other examples and create a list as you did in the previous exercise. Again, give these memories enough time to form.

Your list might look something like this.

Giving Love Is:

Listening carefully

Giving a massage or back rub

Satisfying my partner

Setting aside special time to be together

Giving my spouse a special gift

Stopping what I'm doing to pay attention

Saying "I love you"

Cooking for my family

Taking time out during work to call

Making my partner laugh

Babying my partner when sick

Letting my partner choose the movie, restaurant, or TV show

Making these two lists should give you a clearer picture of love as you experience it. Once you have the two lists, review them, and contrast these characteristics with the kind of relationships you have been having. How well do they match up?

Knowing how you like to give and receive love helps you:

1. Understand what attracted you to your partner in the beginning

2. Express clearly what your wants are so your partner can understand

3. Know when you're receiving love as you recognize it and when your partner is expressing love in his or her own style

4. Redefine your idea of a relationship from what the culture says to what would actually work for you

5. Communicate with your partner, learning to understand each other's needs for how to be loved and for giving love

When you explore and analyze what love means to you in all these ways and then share it, you'll have a much clearer understanding about what love means to each of you and how to show love to each other in ways you'll both understand.

Power in Relationships

When we think of intimate relationships, we usually think of love, but power is also a tremendously important component. In relationships we can learn skills that give us more power to get our needs met, and we can gain understanding that gives us more power to get along with the other people involved. There are three main types of power in relationships: the power of personal space, the power of privacy, and the power of self-control.

Personal Space vs. Closeness

Personal space is difficult to describe. It is the emotional and physical room you need to be comfortable. We all know when we don't have enough: feeling crowded, pressured, and uncomfortable. Intimacy can be compared to food and shelter, because we need it as much. But just as with food and shelter, no one needs it all the time, and some people need more than others. As human beings, we have both a need to belong and a need to be unique. We want to be accepted, to belong, and we also want to be special and recognized as different. These needs often appear to conflict as we search for the balance point between them.

Pressure for Intimacy

It's often surprising to realize that the intimacy that comes with a relationship can be a problem. You or your partner can easily feel stress or pressure about too much closeness and not enough separateness. If you feel you have to cater to or be nice to your partner all the time and put aside what you really want to do (your spouse insists on talking about the relationship when you'd rather just zone out in front of the TV, for example), you'll feel resentful and want to get away from your partner and the related stress.

This problem arises because many of us have hidden "rules" or beliefs about relationships. That is, once we find someone we want to be close to, we feel that we shouldn't ever want to pull away. So to protect our personal space, we put up unconscious barriers, behaviors, and responses that communicate to others, "Go away" or "Don't get too close." Behaving this way, of course, can hurt your partner's feelings and create big problems in the relationship. For example, if you pull away and get quiet or cold, and your partner feels pushed away, doesn't understand it, and panics, then he or she may insist on being reassured by demanding more closeness. This will make your need for space more acute, and you'll pull away further, and your partner will become more demanding. This whole process can lead to struggling, hurt feelings, and anger, and you may not even understand what you're fighting about.

Individual Needs for Personal Space

Your own need for personal space may be a lot different from your partner's, your child's, or others that you know; your spouse's personal space can be a lot different from some previous partner's needs; or the idea of appropriate closeness can be affected by cultural and family styles. For example, eldest or only children usually want more personal space and are more comfortable alone than middle or youngest children or children from big families. This is because eldest/only children are accustomed to spending more time alone than children with lots of siblings.

If you were born in a family whose style was very formal, or a culture, like many Asians, where there is a great deal of respect for each other's space (though they often live very close together), then you'll be horrified if your partner pries into your personal things, walks in on you in the bathroom, reads your mail, asks too many personal questions, or wants a lot of attention.

If, instead, you grew up in a close, very informal family, who had a lot of group activities and interactions, you might be quite comfortable with your spouse being very present, asking lots of questions, and wanting to share everything with you.

No Right or Wrong

Whatever amount of closeness or distance is comfortable for you, even if it's different from your partner's preference, is

OK. There is no right or wrong amount of personal space. The problems that arise are created when couples don't recognize it is natural and normal to be different in personal space requirements. If one of you thinks there's a "rule" about how close a couple should be, or how much privacy one should have, and the two of you differ, then struggles can arise. Understanding your own need for personal space can greatly ease, and even eliminate, this problem. For example, if you are able to explain your needs for space and privacy and to understand your partner's, you may be surprised to find out how different your needs are, and the two of you will have a much better chance of working out agreements that allow you to meet each other's needs.

The Personal Space Solution

If personal space differences are creating problems, they can be fixed through understanding and communication. There are many creative ways to meet different needs, and by acknowledging and meeting each other's needs your relationship will be strengthened. For example:

- If your partner needs more alone time than you do, you can go out for dinner with friends (or join a club, work late, go to the gym or to choir practice) one or two nights a week, while your partner stays home.
- If your partner wants to discuss the relationship a lot, and you don't like to, you can agree to half-hour discussions of the relationship once a week, which will honor your partner's need for discussion and have a limit you can manage.
- If you want lots of friends and family around and your partner is uncomfortable with groups, you can negotiate to spend some time alone with your family or have your family over when your partner isn't home, or you can even be in the living room with everyone while your partner cooks, barbeques, or makes the drinks and keeps some distance.

Accepting that you and your spouse may have differing needs for personal space, learning to identify your own needs and communicate them, and finding out about your partner's needs gives you the information that makes it possible to use the power of personal space to help, rather than hurt, your relationship.

The Power of Privacy

Privacy is your personal power to determine your own internal boundaries and how much of yourself you will share with others. Your private thoughts, your feelings, your personal correspondence, your sexuality, even bathroom time and your clothing are all areas in which you may have higher or lower comfort levels than other people. As with personal space, people have differing needs for privacy because of past history. For example, if you grew up with many siblings or a close extended family that valued sharing, your needs for personal privacy may not be nearly as great as someone who grew up as an only child or in an emotionally distant family. Also, as with personal space, respect for privacy and emotional reticence are highly valued in certain families and cultures.

A Matter of Style

These differences are matters of style—not of right or wrong. Either style, carried to extremes, can become dysfunctional, as when warmth, closeness, and interest become overbearing and smothering or, on the other hand, when respect for privacy and emotional reticence become cold and stifling.

Knowing how to move between the two modes, and having a choice of when and with whom to use each one, is one of the skills that make the difference between relationships that work and people who are in constant conflict.

Different Strokes

We all have different categories of people in our lives. There are family members, friends, co-workers, colleagues, and acquaintances. And within each of these categories there are levels of closeness. In your family, for example, you may feel closer and more comfortable with one sister or cousin than with another. Or in your circle of friends, some may be much more reliable and warm than others. Even in business some colleagues may be true friends while others are more distant.

The differences in these relationships determine how much distance or closeness will work in them. Knowing how to exercise your power of privacy will make a big difference in your couple relationship, and with your friends, extended family, and even business associates.

EXERCISE: Intimacy Inventory

Ask yourself the following questions:

1. Do I prefer to be with other people or alone?
2. If someone else borrowed my clothing, would it feel good, like sharing, or intrusive, as if they were taking advantage of me?
3. Do I like to be with one person at a time, or do I prefer a group?
4. Would I rather talk to someone, listen to him or her, or read to myself?
5. Do I like to talk about my spouse to my friends?
6. Do I like it when my spouse tells friends about me?
7. What limits do I want to set about talking to friends about relationships?

Asking yourself questions of this nature will help you get in touch with how much privacy or closeness you need. Once you know your personal privacy needs, you will be much more aware of when intimacy feels good, and when it doesn't, in your various kinds of relationships.

To learn about the intimacy needs of your mate and other people you know, observe them carefully:

- Who sits or stands closer to you at a party, and who keeps some distance?
- Who shares a lot of personal information, and who keeps personal details secret?
- Who is curious about you; who never asks?
- Who tends to touch people on the shoulder or arm, who hugs, and who never touches except for a handshake?
- Of your co-workers, who is all business, and who likes to have friendly chats?
- Do you know of siblings who share clothing and are always talking about feelings?
- Do you know other siblings who hardly talk?

All these details are clues to the privacy needs of the people around you. If you pay attention, people will demonstrate their tolerance level for intimacy. Once you understand your own needs for privacy, and the difference between your needs and the needs of others, you will find that you can work out privacy issues much more easily in all your relationships. Discussing the power of privacy will make you and your partner more comfortable with each other, and with other people.

The Power of Self-Control

Most people would like to be able to control others—to cause someone to love them, to make someone behave better, to get someone to leave them alone. Unfortunately, it is impossible for any of us to truly control another person. What many people have a tendency to forget is that we have total power to control ourselves, and that if we use this power effectively, we can influence others quite a bit.

The Power of Response

In relationships, most of the interactions are responses. That is, you do something (stimulus); I respond to what you do (response); you respond to my response; I respond to your response; you respond to my response to your response; and so on. There are a few original actions or statements, and all the rest are reactions. This means that if you control your actions and your responses, you control a great deal of the relationship. Your partner and others will usually respond according to what you do.

For a simple illustration of this, imagine I walk into the room, see you, and say, in a disgusted tone of voice, "Oh. It's you," sounding not very pleased to see you. How would you feel, and how would the rest of our interaction go?

Now, imagine that I walk into the room, see you, and say, "How nice to see you," in a really pleased tone, with a big smile. How would you feel then, and how would our interaction go?

Obviously, we are much more likely to have an easy, comfortable time with each other in the second example because my initial action (being glad to see you) set up a better series of responses than if I were clearly not glad to see you.

This simple example illustrates a profound fact: Anyone who is willing to do the work necessary to control his or her emotions, reactions, and responses can control the vast majority of a relationship. We often don't realize how much our reactions contribute to a partner's behavior.

If your partner is angry, for example, and begins to yell, but you keep calm and quiet and just remain there, obviously listening but not reacting, your partner will run out of steam and stop yelling quite quickly, because it feels very uncomfortable to yell if no one is yelling back.

If you take care to speak to your partner and your family in positive, loving ways, and address them directly with kindness, you'll find that very soon they will all begin to be more kind and considerate of you. By controlling your own behavior, you'll influence theirs more than nagging and criticizing ever could.

Learning Self-Control

Maintaining this type of attitude, however, is a lot easier to describe than it is to do. Self-control is not easy. In the face of your partner's actions, it's difficult not to react. Learning to stop and think, to respond *thoughtfully* and *carefully* rather than quickly and automatically, is hard. However, mastering self-control, no matter how difficult, is always worthwhile, because it makes every moment of your life easier.

Using Self-Talk

If learning self-control is difficult for you, one of the most powerful tools you can use to change is self-talk. We all have a running dialogue in our heads, which often is negative or self-defeating. The good news is that you can choose to replace this negative talk with something more positive. The brain tends to repeat familiar things over and over, going again and again over established neuronal pathways. Repeating a mantra, an affirmation, or a choice over and over creates new pathways, which eventually become automatic. The new thoughts will run through your head like the old thoughts did, or like a popular song you've heard over and over.

If your self-talk feels "naturally negative," you may be creating a self-fulfilling identity, which saps your ability to choose your responses. One thing you can do is to monitor your self-talk: What do you say to yourself about the upcoming day, about mistakes, about your luck? If these messages are negative, changing them can indeed lift your spirits and your optimism.

Know yourself: If you love silence, tend to be quiet, and prefer quiet conversations to big parties, this may be a genetic trait—your hearing and nervous system may be more sensitive than most people's, and this trait will not go away. You can, however, make the most of it, and learn that creating plenty of quiet in your life will make you a happier, calmer person. If, on the other hand, you're a party animal—social, enjoying noise and excitement, you can also use that as an asset. Positive, happy people do have an easier time in life and bounce back from problems faster. There are things you can do in every case to increase your level of optimism, even if you can't change who you are.

Your thoughts affect your mood, and how you relate to yourself can either lift or dampen your spirits. Neuronal activity in the brain activates hormones that are synonymous with feelings. Constant self-criticism results in a "what's the use" attitude, which leads to depression and crankiness, which doesn't work well in your marriage. Continuous free-floating thoughts of impending doom lead to anxiety attacks. Negative self-talk creates stress.

What I do to help clients become aware of self-inflicted stress is ask them to become aware of what they're saying to themselves—if there is a constant stream of negativity, it will create stress, just as being followed around by someone who's constantly carping at you would be stressful. Also, if they're fighting within themselves—not able to come to a solid idea of what they want—that will make it difficult to make decisions and increase the stress. Dysfunctional relationship patterns also are stress building. For example, if you are constantly guilt-tripped by someone, or you and your spouse fight, or you are too worried about others' opinions of who you are and what you're doing, you'll be a lot more stressed than if you know how to get along with others and when to listen and when to trust yourself. Most of my clients don't realize that they are responsible for their own feelings, and no one else is responsible for making them feel better.

To move from powerless about yourself to being in charge, try the following suggestions:

- **Make a note:** Write positive comments on your daily calendar to yourself for jobs well done or any achievements you want to celebrate. Or you can paste stickers on your daily calendar as you accomplish goals; daily, frequent positive commentary is a very effective way to reward yourself and remind yourself of your success.
- **Look to your childhood:** Use activities that felt like a celebration in your childhood. Did your family toast a celebration with champagne or sparkling cider, a gathering of friends, or a thankful prayer? Create a celebration environment: Use balloons, music, flowers, candles, or set your table with the best china.
- **Visible reminders:** Surround yourself with visible evidence of your successes. Plant a commemorative rosebush or get a new houseplant to mark a job well done, or display photos of fun events and sports or hobby trophies. It's a constant reminder that you appreciate yourself and when you see them daily, you'll feel the appreciation.
- **Reward yourself:** A new trashy romance novel or detective thriller can be a great reward/celebration for reading your required technical books.
- **Party:** Celebrate a success or solving a problem with an impromptu lunchtime picnic and a balloon, or with tickets to a ball game.

Chapter 9

COUPLES COUNSELING

In my thirty-five years as a licensed psychotherapist I have counseled many couples, and it's very gratifying to see them change and grow and even restore marriages they thought were over. It makes my day when I open my e-mail and get a message from a client that says, "Dear Dr. Tessina: Thank you so much. I have my husband back.—J"

Twenty-five years ago, at the beginning of my own marriage, because my husband and I had both been through previous painful divorces, we made a deal: We'd go for a counseling session if we couldn't solve a problem together within three days. In the early years, we did indeed go for counseling a number of times, and we only needed a session or two to solve whatever problem seemed too difficult for us. We laugh now to remember that it soon only took one of us to say "We need a counseling session!" to get us to stop being silly and solve the problem.

Marriage counseling is a gift, a wonderful resource distilled from the work of some of the world's greatest thinkers, clinicians, and philosophers. When I first began my practice, the theories of family and couples counseling were in their infancy, with such exciting pioneers as Virginia Satir showing us how effective couples counseling techniques could be. It was a privilege to learn from her, from Carl Rogers, Abraham Maslow, Thomas Szasz, Fritz Perls, Ken Keyes, Albert Ellis, and my mentor, Denton Roberts. Today, there is an abundance of research, clinical work, and writing from innovators such as John Gottman, Ellen Langer, Melody Beattie, John Bradshaw, Mihaly Czikszentmihalyi, and James Hillman, which has created a new "technology of relationships" that underlies and informs my own experience in the counseling office.

Because we have all this great research, and counseling is now so effective, it always surprises me when I hear that people are resisting going to counseling or dread it. It is sad when people who would benefit from counseling shy away and avoid it.

Many people have misconceptions about marital counseling. To set the record straight:

- It's not a punishment for being bad.
- It's not a "gotcha" session, where you are blamed and called wrong.
- It's not too expensive (if you go early, it only takes a session or two—if you wait five years, it takes a lot longer).
- It's not "airing your dirty laundry"—all sessions are completely confidential, and private. The counselor is required by law not to tell anything you said in the session without your permission.
- It's not a way to lose or win an argument. A competent counselor will not take sides; he or she will help you stop struggling and start communicating.
- It's not proof that there's something wrong with you.
- It does not require both partners—if your partner will not go with you, go alone.
- It does not usually lead to divorce. The earlier you go, the more likely your marriage can be repaired.

- It will not make you unhappy. In fact, if your marriage is not happy, marriage counseling can help you learn to have fun together.
- It does not have to be about sex. While there are counselors whose specialty is sexual issues, most counselors focus mostly on problem-solving and communication skills (which can also help your sex life).
- It can teach you skills like the ones in this book to help you work together better. (In fact, this book can be used as a manual for couples in counseling.)
- It can help you handle a specific problem, such as a difficult relative, boss, or child, or an addiction or behavior problem.
- It can help you survive stress and trauma that otherwise might ruin your marriage, such as the death of a child or a parent, the loss of a job, or serious health problems.
- It can help you prepare for many life transitions, such as moving a long distance, changing careers, dealing with an "empty nest" when the children grow up, blending families after remarriage, and retirement.
- It can help you make big decisions that will affect your future, such as whether to get married or have children, when to retire, how to help an aging parent, or whether to buy a home.
- It can help you handle a big change in your relationship, such as handling a temporary separation due to career changes, military deployment, or jobs that take you away from home frequently.

There is no rational reason to avoid going for counseling. If you think you need it, go. It will help.

Resentment and Tenacious Problems

Throughout this book I have mentioned the destructive power of resentment many times because it can be such a detrimental force in marriage. Couples who don't want to hurt each other's feelings can avoid talking about things they don't like and wind up with a stockpile of resentment. For a while, you can avoid facing problems directly by not saying anything about what's bothering you, but when you do that, you'll store up resentment about it. This may seem easier than direct talk for a while, but you'll find there's a big price to pay for avoiding discussion. Resentment is the great destroyer of love. You can be angry at each other or have hurt feelings, and if you talk about the problem, your feelings will be resolved and your love will be intact. But if you instead brood and nurse your resentment and anger, you'll begin to see your partner as a problem rather than a supportive person.

Whenever you realize you feel resentment toward your partner, speak up right away. If the two of you can't solve the problem within a day or two, go for counseling. One session at the beginning of a problem will save you the many sessions you'll need if you stay angry at each other for a long time. Use the following guidelines to find couples counseling that will help you sort out problems you can't solve by yourselves.

Guidelines for Finding and Using Therapy Wisely

When to look for a therapist:

1. You have problems, either as individuals or as a couple, that you can't solve by yourself or by talking to friends and family.

2. You cannot control such behaviors as temper tantrums, alcohol or drug addiction, painful relationships, anxiety attacks, or depression.

3. You have serious difficulties communicating in your relationships.

4. You have sexual problems or sexual dysfunction that does not go away by itself.

5. You or your partner become verbally or physically violent or abusive (even once).

6. One or both of you have a general, pervasive unhappiness with your life.

7. You and your partner have disagreements and struggles you can't resolve yourselves.

8. Your partner keeps telling you something's wrong with your relationship, but you don't believe it's true (or you're trying to tell your partner there's a problem and he or she won't listen).

Where to Look for a Therapist

Finding a counselor is easy. Licensed counselors of every sort exist everywhere, and they can be found in the phone book or via an online search. Finding the *right* counselor is harder, but critically important to your success in counseling. Like lawyers, plumbers, or doctors, the quality of counselors and therapists can vary. You need a referral or recommendation of an effective, suitable, and experienced counselor in your area. There are several sources that are good, depending on what's available to you:

- **Advertising:** This is the least dependable source for the right counselor because you usually cannot tell from an ad whether the counselor has had the proper training for your issues or whether you'll feel good about him or her. If you don't have a referral from someone you know, you can interview therapists by phone as the guidelines below show you, and choose the best one.
- **Hotlines:** Even if you are not suicidal or a domestic violence or rape victim, you can call a local hotline. Most of them will refer you to a counselor or clinic in your area.

These hotlines often know the counselors personally—you can ask how they screen their referrals. Hotline staff are well trained and know the resources in your area. Look in the front pages of your phone book for a list of hotlines.

- **Internet search:** If you have access to online searching, you can find a lot of therapists on the Internet. Look for online groups that specialize in your issues, such as depression, anxiety, addiction, or relationships.

- **Nonprofit professional associations:** Associations of counselors and therapists can refer you to a therapist in your area that has met the organization's qualifications. This is especially important if you live in an area where counselors are not licensed. Try the Association for Humanistic Psychology (*www.ahp.org*), the American Association for Marriage Family Therapists (*www.aamft.org*), or the American Psychotherapy Association (*www.american psychotherapy.com*). Such nonprofit organizations are also listed in the phone book and directory assistance, with branches in major cities.

- **Referrals from friends:** The best source for a good counselor is probably referrals from friends who have seen a counselor and can tell you firsthand that he or she is competent, friendly, and effective. Any counselor who is recommended by someone you know will most likely be your best bet.

Find a counselor who is supportive and understanding and with whom you are comfortable. If you don't, you will be less open and forthcoming about your problems and your counselor will be less helpful. To see a counselor and withhold information is the equivalent of taking your car to a mechanic and giving him false information about what's wrong. The counselor, like the mechanic, is liable to focus on fixing the wrong thing.

A good, knowledgeable counselor will be informative and helpful when you call to ask for information and will gladly explain the counseling process to you. He or she will also be willing to answer any questions you have about the counseling process at any time and will lead you step-by-step through the procedure.

What to Expect from a Counseling Session

Knowing how a session should go will help you maximize the benefits of counseling and also prevent potential problems.

So far, so good. You've decided to seek counseling, found a referral, and now you're facing the moment of truth—calling for an appointment. There is no need to be afraid of this. If this is a counselor who's been personally recommended, you have an excellent chance that you've found someone good. If you got the name from other sources, then it's up to you to check your chosen professional out. Here's how to go about it.

Interviewing a Therapist

Normally, you will call the counselor first for an appointment. If you know in advance what you'd like to find out about the counselor, you can take charge of the phone conversation and make sure you find out as much about him or her as he or she does about you.

There are several things you will want to know in advance:

- **Expertise:** Is the counselor licensed? What is his or her area of expertise? Does he or she work with depression, anxiety, recovery, or whatever issues you want to focus on? If it's a couple problem, does the therapist do couples' therapy?
- **Price:** How long is a session? What is her rate and is there a sliding scale?
- **Payment:** Will he take a check, a credit card, does he take your insurance, are there charges for filling out insurance

papers, do you pay in advance and have insurance reimburse you, or does he get paid by them directly?

- **Hours:** Does she recommend how often you come in, or can you set the frequency of visits according to your needs, finances, and work schedule? Does she see clients on nights or weekends?

- **Duration:** Does this counselor do long-term or short-term therapy? Not very long ago, most therapy was very intensive and took years to complete, but today's therapy techniques can handle your immediate problems in just a few sessions, especially if you have done the exercises in this book, and already have an understanding of what you might need to work on.

Phone Interview

If a receptionist or a secretary answers when you phone a therapist, ask to speak directly with the counselor. Most often, the therapist will be "in session"—counseling someone—when you call and will not be able to take your call immediately, but he can call you back if you leave a message that says *specifically* when you're available (i.e., "after 6:00 in the evening" or "Saturday all day"). Alternatively, you can find out when he is available to take calls and call back then. Some counselors will offer a free or low-cost initial interview in which you can ask questions and find out details. Keep calling and interviewing therapists until the above questions have been answered to your satisfaction, and then make an appointment.

The First Session

When you go into the office, you will probably be given forms to fill out, as in a medical doctor's office. There are several reasons for this:

1. The counselor will need to get the necessary information for filling out insurance forms (name, address, social security number, date of birth, nature of problem, name and number of your medical doctor).

2. The counselor seeks to learn some facts about you that will help in counseling (family history, marital history, any previous hospitalizations for mental illness, current medications, and previous therapy).

3. The therapist will keep this information in a file on you and your progress. Although it is rare, a court can subpoena these records, so don't answer any questions you find uncomfortable. Give your answers verbally to the counselor instead, and explain that you don't want them written down because you want your privacy protected. Don't be too worried about this, however; your counselor will not divulge information unless a court requires him to, but you have a right to know what is and is not protected information.

Once the forms are filled out, your counselor will see you in her office and the session will begin. The first session is called an intake session, which is an initial interview. If you have a clear idea of what the problem is before you go in, your counselor will be more effective. You will probably be asked what is wrong, what you have tried to do to fix it, and how you think it should be resolved. A good counselor will be neutral and helpful and may offer suggestions or even give you "homework" (an exercise to do between sessions), but he should not impose his beliefs or ideas on you.

If you felt good about your counselor on the phone, this session should verify that you are in knowledgeable hands. If you can see in the first few sessions that the therapy will be helpful and you're learning new things, you're probably in the right place.

Therapist Statement of Ethics

This is the statement of ethics published by the American Psychotherapy Association for their members to hand out to their clients. Other professional associations have similar codes. I reproduce it here to give you an idea of ethical counseling behavior.

As a Psychotherapist:
- I must first do no harm.
- I will promote healing and well-being in my clients and place the clients and public's interests above my own at all times.
- I will respect the dignity of the persons with whom I am working, and I will remain objective in my relationships with clients' and will act with integrity in dealing with other professionals.
- I will provide only those services for which I have had the appropriate training and experience and will keep my technical competency at the highest level in order to uphold professional standards of practice.
- I will not violate the physical boundaries of the client and will always provide a safe and trusting haven for healing.
- I will defend the profession against unjust criticism and defend colleagues against unjust actions.
- I will seek to improve and expand my knowledge through continuing education and training.
- I will refrain from any conduct that would reflect adversely upon the best interest of the American Psychotherapy Association and its ethical standard of practice.

A counselor or therapist who adheres to this or a similar code will behave ethically and be an effective help in your search to demystify your past.

Whether you do your search to demystify your past by yourself or use the help of a therapist, you'll find that the information concealed in your own mind is fascinating and valuable.

Chapter 10

LOVE WITHOUT STRUGGLES

Before you got married, I'm sure you had a rosy picture of your future life together. I know you never intended to spend your time struggling. However, as with most dreams of the future, when reality set in, it may have looked a lot different from your early expectations. The good news is it's not too late to create that wonderful life you dreamed of. You and your partner now have the tools you need to create a harmonious partnership and to feel lucky to be facing the problems of life together and have each other through good and bad. This chapter will show you some additional tools and enhancements to make a good marriage even better.

State of the Union Meeting

We discussed having a regular family meeting in chapter 4 (page 114), but it is equally valuable to have couple meetings without other family members. For any married couple, having a regular weekly meeting date to discuss the state of the relationship will make a tremendous difference in the emotional tenor of the relationship. In my counseling practice, I watch couples' relationships improve dramatically from just this one technique. Keeping to a regular schedule will help you become so familiar with the process that discussions at any other time also become much easier. Regularly talking about what's going on sets a pattern of open communication that will support you as a couple through any problems that arise.

When you have a regular chance to talk about what's going on in the relationship, problems, resentment, and frustration don't get a chance to build. Regular couple meetings, where both of you express feelings, negative and positive, and you work together to solve problems establishes a rational, functional basis for all marital business.

If you set a pattern of doing this early in a relationship, the formality of the meeting will soon relax, problems will be minor, and the two of you can use the time for bonding, sharing stories and experiences, and creating quality time together.

Steps for State of the Union Meetings

1. Gratitude: Each of you states a positive thing about the other, preferably something that has happened this week. For example, "I really appreciate how much you helped me this week when you knew I had a deadline at work." Or, "I noticed that you made a big effort to keep the kitchen clean." Or, "Thank you for your sense of humor. It really helps when you make me laugh when I'm getting too serious." Be sure to thank your spouse after praising him or her. If you follow a religious tradition, you can begin by giving thanks in the manner of your faith.

2. Improvements: Each of you then mentions anything you want to improve and what you think will solve the problem. The rule is that in order to bring up a complaint you must have a suggestion for a solution, even if you don't think it's the best possible solution.

3. Problem Solving: If either of you has a problem to solve, he or she can describe it, and then you work together to come up with a solution. Be careful not to allow the description of the problem to deteriorate into criticism and complaining. To state a problem use fact-based terms rather than emotional drama, and use "I" messages: "I'm discouraged and frustrated because the house is so messy." "We need to come up with some money to fix the car." "I have a problem at work." "I think we're over-scheduled this weekend."

This simple meeting will do more for the state of your intimate relationship than you can imagine. If you deal with problems as they arise, and approach them with a team spirit of solving them together, most of them can be solved before they become disasters.

Relationship Reservoir

These meetings will accomplish a great deal, and can change the nature of what I call your "relationship reservoir": Every relationship (including family, friends, and parent/child relationships) has what I call a "relationship reservoir." Over the course of your relationships, the interactions between you and your friends and intimates—every kind or unkind word, every gesture of support or criticism, every honest or dishonest communication between you, every gesture of affection or coldness—adds up to a reservoir of feelings and attitudes.

Filling Your Reservoir

If you fill your reservoir with good feelings, forgiveness, support, honesty, appreciation, caring, affection, and emotional intimacy (and sexual intimacy where appropriate), you will build up a backlog of goodwill and affection and your memories will be warm and mutually admiring.

If you fill it with coldness, criticism, ingratitude, dishonesty, demands, and dissatisfaction, you'll have a reservoir of resentment and disdain.

Each time your relationship makes demands on you as a result of major problems, separations, disagreements, illnesses, and stress, you will draw on your relationship reservoir. If you have built up a supply of good feelings and goodwill with your daily interaction, you'll cheerfully give what's asked of you. If not, whatever's asked will seem like too much to give.

I wish you a reservoir overflowing with warmth and good feelings—the true guarantee of a lasting relationship.

Create a Marriage Journal

To create a tangible picture of the positive things in your reservoir, create a marriage journal. It will become a positive reinforcement for your entire marriage. Get a large scrapbook, the type that allows you to add more pages later. Choose the cover carefully to reflect your mutual goals for your marriage. Begin the scrapbook with a few (no more than four or five) highlights from your wedding. Choose only the most memorable moments. Your marriage journal is for the highlights, the most significant moments of your life together. You already have your wedding album and video to remember the small details of the wedding, as well as an album of pictures from your honeymoon. Using just a few pictures, make a page about your honeymoon. You can write notes about the most romantic moments, where you ate, what you did. Take a picture of the bed in your hotel room and add it to the journal. Throughout your married life, you can continue to add significant moments to your journal. Paste in an anniversary card, two or three pictures of each vacation, a picture of your new home, each baby or new pet when it arrives, mementos of career achievements, holiday group photos, children's artwork, and love notes to each other. When you have children, it becomes a family journal.

Throughout your life together, when you need encouragement, you can pull this book out and look at it together. Not only will it make each occasion memorable, but also each new page will remind you of all the important milestones you have shared together. As this book grows, it will become one of your most precious possessions, a tangible expression of the power and joy in your marriage.

Use your marriage journal whenever you need to be reassured that your marriage is worth the struggle; to help your children understand what happened to mom and dad before the children were born; to celebrate occasions, big and small, in the life of your family.

Staying Together

The skills couples need to keep intimacy alive in a long-term relationship differ from new relationship intimacy skills, and learning them is not automatic, because people don't talk about them. Basically, as a couple you need to lower your expectations of romance and glamour and raise the level of fun and happiness you have together. Regular weekly talks keep the problems minor, the resentment level down, and the communication open, so that there is time and space for intimacy. In a successful, long-term relationship, passion becomes a shared sense of humor and goodwill toward each other.

Because your relationship is a reflection of the attitudes and experience of both of you, it must change as you do to be sustainable. These continuous changes, whether caused by circumstances (a new job means you must move to a new city), personal growth (you become more self-assured, and want to make some new friends or develop a talent), or an unexpected event (your spouse gets a serious illness), always create some turmoil and confusion, but if you understand how to work together, the disruption is minimal, and you get maximum enjoyment.

Unless you've been through a very long-term relationship before, it's hard to understand the changes that will be necessary as your relationship develops because we tend to think once we get along, it will last forever. Understanding that your relationship continues to go through growing phases throughout your life together will help a lot.

One thing that grows and changes as your relationship progresses is love. In chapter 8 you explored how giving and receiving love feels. Here we'll explore the more philosophical side of love.

Aspects of Love

Many couples come to me confused about love, and they're not alone. What rapturous, torturous words have been set down to try and capture the essence of love. Those clever Greeks, who invented the Olympics, also believed in many gods who governed and represented the many components of love—Aphrodite, Dionysus, Eros, and Hestia. Aphrodite was prayed to as the goddess of love and beauty, and Eros was responsible for lust and sex. Dionysus embodied liberation through ecstasy (and wine), and Hestia was prayed to for fertility. A different god was responsible for the different parts of this crazy thing we call love.

These clever Greeks had several words for several categories of love as well. They did not attempt to squeeze all of it into four little letters! *Eros* was erotic, or sexual love; *philos* was brotherly love; *agape* was altruistic, spiritual love. The Latin poet Ovid spoke of *amor ludens*, or playful love—love as a game. Having separate categories like these can be very helpful in thinking and talking about how you love. In modern times, we speak of romantic love, mature love, parental love, innocent childlike love, friendship, and even intellectual love. And why not circumstantial love for those we become fond of because we're thrown together at work or some other activity—even though the relationship or friendship doesn't last once the circumstance changes? A workplace friendship might be in that category.

Ask ten people what love is and you'll get ten different answers. Ask those same people how they want to be loved—and each one will want something unique. One wants to be given space, another wants constant companionship. To be held and touched sounds great to some, smothering to others. There is no way we can know how to love each other without communicating about it.

Love's home is the heart, and love is not limited to one type or expression. There is plenty to go around, and the more of it we share, the more we have. You have to let someone know how you feel if you want your love to be returned. Expressing how you feel is taking a risk, but I think it's even riskier not to express yourself.

To find out what love is, it's best to ask your heart, which always knows when you feel abused and when someone is too demanding. You may not like the answer, but you can recognize it for the truth. When I listen to my heart, I can stop worrying, because my heart is surprisingly in tune with one of the world's oldest definitions of love: "Love is patient and kind; love is neither jealous nor boastful; it is not arrogant or rude" (St. Paul). "Love does not insist on its own way; it is not irritable or resentful; it does not rejoice at wrong, but rejoices in the right." Whether I'm receiving love or giving it, the "real thing" fits that description. The interesting thing is, when I give love away instead of hoarding it, I always seem to receive more than I can possibly give.

Love can certainly be painful, and experiencing both the joy and pain of it changes us, as I expressed in this poem:

Mosaic Heart

A fully living heart

In the passing of time

And love, and loss

Breaks and stretches

Heals and shatters.

Striated, scarred,

Misshapen, resilient

Until finally it assimilates

Its wounds and calluses

Into character.

A rare glimpse of this mosaic

(deep in eyes opened in surrender)

Reveals the soul's holy icon

Inscribed on the flesh

Inspired by love

Born of attachment and release

Colored in bits of joy and pain.

Try feeling the love in your heart, and once you're clear on what aspect of love you feel in a given situation, you can begin to communicate it.

The following guidelines will help you sort out this deeply perplexing emotion.

Guidelines for Relating with Love
(Six Things to Remember)

1. It's not about who's right or wrong; it's about solving the problem together. If you try to win the argument, you'll lose something more important—loving feelings.

2. With listening, caring, and the willingness to change, anything in your relationship can be fixed. There's no need to be afraid; just turn up the love.

3. It's a partnership, silly! Stop struggling, and learn to work together. Focus on teamwork and sharing.

4. Behavior that enhances relationships with people at work and with your friends will probably work if you use it with your spouse. Seek to be more rational and less angry or emotional.

5. What goes around comes around, in love as well as life. If you want more of love, try giving more. It will work every time.

6. Be a grownup, not a little kid. Think before you speak, and focus on solutions, not problems. Give up whining, complaining, and suffering, and step up to taking responsibility and loving more.

All of us want to be irresistible to our partners, to be loved without hesitation, fully and deeply. The following guidelines will help you melt any resistance your partner may have to letting his or her love shine through to you.

Guidelines for Being Irresistible to Your Mate

1. Don't resist, listen. We often have a knee-jerk negative response to what a mate tells us, or wants to do. Instead of replying negatively ("That won't work..." "We can't do that...\"), try listening and thinking for a few seconds more. You may find out your initial response changes, and at any rate, listening and understanding is not the same as agreeing. When your spouse feels that you care about what he or she is saying, the nature of the communication will change for the better.

2. Look your mate in the eyes and smile. Unless your partner is talking about something really sad (job loss, death, etc.), where a smile would be inappropriate, look him or her in the eyes and smile while you're listening. Your companion will automatically feel more understood and cared about, which will change the feeling level of the discussion. This doesn't mean to stare unblinkingly, but just to look frequently for a few seconds at a time, to communicate your attentiveness.

3. Touch each other. Sit near your significant other, and gently place your hand on his or her shoulder, leg, or arm. If you're in the car, lightly touch his or her shoulder or arm. You'll find your conversation becomes warmer and more caring. If you've been struggling, or are ready to forgive each other, facing each other and holding both hands will help you feel more positively connected and reassured.

4. Try laughter. If something frustrating is happening, try easing the tension with a bit of humor. After a difficult interaction in a store, on the way out, you could say, "That went well," with a touch of irony. Or, when someone drops something and makes a mess, you could say, "the gremlins are here again." Or use comedienne Gilda Radner's line "It's always something" or Judy Tenuta's "It could happen" to change stress to silliness. Don't poke fun at your mate, but use shared humor as a way to say, "I know this is tough, but we'll get through it." Your mate will think of you as someone soothing and helpful to have around when problems happen.

5. Use pleasant surprises. Try a love note in your spouse's briefcase; a post-it with a smiley face on the underside of the toilet seat; a flower, plant, card, or balloon for no reason; or an unexpected gentle pat on the rear, a hug, or a kiss to say "I'm thinking good thoughts about you, and I love you."

6. Ramp up the sweetness. Married life has its unavoidable stresses and strains. To keep things in balance, we need to put a bit of energy into increasing the sweetness between us. Thoughtfulness, "thank-yous," and gestures of politeness and affection are the WD-40 of your marriage. Keep things running smoothly by remembering to add a spritz of sweetness frequently. You'll be amazed at how good you feel and how much more responsive your partner is.

7. Devote time to your marriage. No matter how crazed you are with work, kids, and bills, it's essential to put aside regular time each week for the marriage. Have a "date night" that includes a "state of the union" discussion (as described above, but just the two of you) or take a pleasant walk or drive. Keeping connected means things don't build up to fighting status, and you'll remember how good you are together. Don't forget to celebrate and appreciate each other. Motivation comes from celebration and appreciation, so when you spend pleasant time together, you'll both be more motivated to make your marriage as good as possible.

8. Focus on partnership. Remember that first and foremost, before anything else, you're partners. Keep that in mind and check frequently to make sure you're acting like partners, and not competitors or avoiders. You're in this thing together, and partnership is what it's all about.

9. Reminisce about good times. "Remember when . . ." is a great beginning to a loving conversation. It creates so much good feeling to remember how you were when you were dating, when you got married, when you first bought your house, when you had your first child, when you got that promotion. Reminding yourselves of your solid history together is a way to increase your bond.

10. Brag to friends in your mate's hearing. Of course, tell your mate to his or her face how much you care, but also be sure to tell your friends, while your mate is around, what a great guy or gal you married. "Harold is so thoughtful. Today he helped me around the house." Or "Sue is such a great mom. She really gives the kids a sense that they're loved and she still keeps them toeing the mark." Or, "Did you hear? Fred got a big promotion. I'm so proud of him." Or, "I don't know what I'd do without Judy. She's so great with money." Or, "Doesn't my sweetie look great today? I'm so lucky." Don't worry if your partner looks embarrassed. He or she will also be pleased and remember your brag for a long time.

Try the Silly Solution for a Healthy Relationship

Early in my marriage, after a difficult struggle between us, I gave my husband a card. All over the front it said, "I love you," and inside it said, "It's a dirty job, but someone has to do it." That phrase has carried us through many difficult times since.

I read many articles about what happens "after the passion dies" in long-term relationships, and my clients frequently are worried about the same question. I believe what happens, when all goes well, is that a sense of humor sets in.

The burden of passion can be a heavy one. Having to rev up the energy for a passionate, heavy-breathing session making love after a hard day's work can be an appalling prospect. How much more inviting it is to be able to have a silly giggle session, complete with sexual play, with the dearest person I know. Suddenly, the heaviness and obligation are gone, and if I'm too tired to be passionate and alluring, I always seem to have the energy to "mess around."

Arguments are hard to have with a lovable three-year-old, which is what my husband can become at the drop of an accusation. He puts his hands on his hips, sticks out his chin, and (in a perfect imitation of a kid mimicking an angry parent) says, "Who did that?" He then points his finger at whatever offense (a messy table, a forgotten chore) I've lost my sense of humor about. Watching him, I can't hang on to my anger.

After we laugh, then we can do something constructive about the problem.

Please understand that I'm speaking of humor, not irresponsibility. We are both adults, entrepreneurs, and we have an equal, relatively balanced relationship. We hashed that out many years ago. We get angry at each other mostly out of irritability, exhaustion, and frustration with our heavy schedules—not because either one of us is slacking off. Things don't get done at times because we have hectic lives, and hectic lives benefit greatly from a sense of humor.

I guess it takes a certain amount of self-acceptance to create healthy humor, rather than the hurtful kind, but then again, this loving, shared laughter has also enhanced my degree of self-acceptance. The paradox seems to be that having permission for childlike play also gives permission to be responsible and self-accepting. We don't make nasty jokes about each other and our love, and I don't exactly know how to express the difference. What I do know is we laugh together, and it feels good to both of us.

We have been together twenty-five years, and I still don't feel in danger of being bored. I seem to easily run out of things to be passionate about, or dramatic about, but laughter never gets boring. It's also difficult to store up resentments against the person in my life who makes it easiest for me to laugh.

I find myself looking for ways to make Richard laugh, and the more I practice it, the better I get. He seems to be getting to know my "laugh buttons" better, too. Could he be looking for them? I wouldn't be surprised.

So, rather than treasuring old grudges, old hurts, we treasure old jokes and funny lines. I know I can turn to Richard and say, "It's a dirty job ..." and get an answering smile. I also know he understands, when I say that phrase, that I love him, "warts and all." It's a good feeling.

There are times when an overwhelming feeling of warmth and caring flows over me, and many of those times are when I laugh with Richard. Humor seems to be the secret, at least for us, in both keeping our love fresh and alive and in feeling confident that we will not lose our specialness to each other.

The more we learn about living together, the less we struggle, and the less we struggle, the more we laugh and play. One of the things I have learned as a therapist is that struggle is often used by families to structure time. As a partner in this relationship, I have learned that replacing the drama of struggle with the delight of humor can be a positive addiction and a powerful solution for what to do with our time together.

The net result of all this is that I have become an advocate of the "silly solution," and it is working better than all the seriousness I used to think my relationships required.

I hope this book has helped you both to take the partnership aspect of your marriage seriously and to lighten up and have more fun together. I know that a marriage failure is devastating, because I went through it myself. I also know that I have since learned the skills and tools I needed both to make my own marriage a success and to help many other people improve their relationships. I know you can do it, too. You can create a good marriage that improves with time. Problems that were once unsolvable can become welcome opportunities to learn and grow. Conflicts will be transformed into negotiations, and laughter, intimacy, and romance will replace struggle and frustration. Instead of yelling, squabbling, and arguing, you can discuss solutions, compare your ideas, and come up with newer, better ideas together—better than either of you can create alone. This is the true meaning of the proverb "two heads are better than one." Both of you will be able to think more clearly and help each other be more creative and resourceful when you're not butting your heads together. The most powerful improvement you can make in your marriage is to learn new skills wherever your old habits aren't working. Once you have learned the new techniques, don't forget to use them over and over. If they work for you once, they'll work again and again. You can come back to the exercises in this book as many times as you need to, until they are second nature to you and the new habits replace the old. With the exercises and guidelines you've learned here, you can create the partnership you want: a reliable, loving, and companionable marriage that helps you see each other through all the ups and downs of life. I wish for you the joy of laughing together and playing with problems until you find a silly solution. May you be blessed with marital joy and a long, happy life together.

INDEX

ABOUT THE AUTHOR

Tina B. Tessina, PhD, MFT, ASJA (*www.tinatessina.com*), is a licensed psychotherapist in private practice in California since 1979. Her practice includes individual and couples counseling. She earned both her BA and MA at the Lindenwood College, St. Charles, Missouri (1977), and her PhD at Pacific Western University, Los Angeles (1987). She is a diplomate of the American Psychotherapy Association and a certified domestic violence counselor, and is certified to supervise counseling interns.

She is the author of eleven books, including: *The 10 Smartest Decisions a Woman Can Make Before 40* and *The Unofficial Guide to Dating Again*. Her most recent books are *It Ends with You: Grow Up and Out of Dysfunction* (2003), *How to Be a Couple and Still Be Free* (2002), and *The Real Thirteenth Step* (2001). Dr. Tessina has appeared extensively on radio and TV, including *To Tell the Truth*, *Larry King Live*, *Oprah*, and *ABC-TV News*. She has been quoted in *Glamour*, *Cosmopolitan*, *O: The Oprah Magazine*, *Ladies Home Journal*, and many other magazines and newspapers and has been published in fourteen languages. On the Internet, she is known as "Dr. Romance," the "Dating Doctor," and "The Love Doctor." She is an online expert who answers relationship questions at *www.CouplesCompany.com*

and on Yahoo!Personals. She is a Redbook Love Network expert and she has been a "Psychology Smarts" columnist for *First for Women*. She publishes the "Happiness Tips from Tina" e-mail newsletter and has hosted *The Psyche Deli: Delectable Tidbits for the Subconscious* radio show. She also writes the "Dr. Romance Blog" at *http://drromance.typepad.com/dr_romance_blog/*.

In addition to her professional work, Dr. Tessina is a trained lyric coloratura soprano. She also writes poetry and song lyrics (which have been recorded by Helen Reddy and others), speaks Spanish and some French, and loves ballroom dancing. She has lived in Long Beach, California, since 1982 with her husband of twenty-five years, Richard Sharrard, ballroom instructor and owner of the Dance Factory. Tina and Richard went around the world in 1998 as dance instructors on the *Crystal Symphony* cruise ship. They spend the little spare time they have traveling, enjoying their 1918 California bungalow, gardening, and playing with their three dogs.